8.00

INVITATION TO FAITH

Christian Belief Today

PAUL JERSILD

AUGSBURG Publishing House • Minneapolis

INVITATION TO FAITH

Copyright © 1978 Augsburg Publishing House

Library of Congress Catalog Card No. 77-84097

International Standard Book No. 0-8066-1623-7 paper
0-8066-1622-9 cloth

Scripture quotations unless otherwise noted are from the Revised Standard Version of the Bible, copyright 1946, 1952, and 1971 by the Division of Christian Education of the National Council of Churches.

MANUFACTURED IN THE UNITED STATES OF AMERICA

For our children
Ann
Austin
Amy
Aaron

Preface

THIS BOOK HAS BEEN WRITTEN primarily for three kinds of readers. It is intended to provide an introduction to Christian teachings for those who feel they are ignorant about the subject and are curious to know more. It may be that their knowledge is limited to impressions from childhood contact with the church, and an occasional sermon or tract. Their relation to the church, in any event, has never been strong.

A second group I find quite often in my college classroom. They are curious about what Christianity can mean to them but are indifferent if not hostile toward the church as a religious institution. They regard themselves as standing at best on the periphery of the church, related to it by family tradition but never having found a meaningful commitment for themselves in what the church has taught them. Their knowledge of Christian teaching is often a collection of doctrines which they know they *cannot* believe, and they wonder if there is anything in the faith of their families that they *can* believe.

A third group to whom this book is directed are those who do identify themselves with the church, but have now come to a point where they feel the need of deepening their understanding of Christian theology. They have become dissatisfied with their impressions of certain teachings of the church which till now they had accepted with little thought. Life involves growth, and many Christians are discovering that their understanding of their faith has not grown but has petrified back at a much earlier age. New insights and perspectives are needed to express the meaning of Christian faith in a way that is adequate for where they are today.

9

With these readers in mind, I have attempted to write this book as one who stands at the door of the church, listening and attempting to respond to the reservations and questions of those who are hesitant to enter that door—or who are sitting rather uneasily inside. To some my presentation of Christian teaching may appear conservative and oblivious to the questions they are raising. To others it may appear that I am playing fast and loose with the church's theological tradition as I interpret it for today. To respond cogently to the questions of every reader is of course more than I can expect. I hope that what I have written will at least be helpful and informative to many, stimulating some further reading and reflection. The annotated bibliography at the end of the book will provide some direction for those interested in pursuing further a particular topic.

My own perspective of Christianity is largely shaped by the Reformation tradition. However, as a Lutheran theologian presently teaching in an ecumenical faculty at a Roman Catholic institution, the reader will correctly surmise that I am most interested in the catholic (universal) substance of Christian faith which unites all Christians, whatever their particular tradition or whatever the theological issues on which they may disagree. This is not to deny that theological differences can be significant, but they are nonetheless differences within the family. It is this fact which often makes disagreements all the more intense! Throughout this book I will have occasion to note differences between Roman Catholic and Protestant traditions in their understanding of particular doctrines or in their approach to certain theological issues.

Since it is an introduction to Christian teaching, this book reflects in its chapter headings the divisions which are common to most presentations of Christian theology. Because of my particular purpose, however, this is not a dogmatics text which seeks to address every facet of Christian doctrine. Essential teachings are presented, but within what theologians call an "apologetic" framework, which means that the approach is sensitive to the questions which people are raising about the Christian faith. There is really no other way that one can discuss theology these days, living as we do in an age which is experiencing a crisis concerning the reality or unreality of God. Such a fundamental problem places everything about Christianity in question, creating a new situation in which one "does theology." It is a temptation for theologians under these circumstances to run off in different directions to find some minor theme which appears *au courant* and to forget about the fundamental task of interpreting the Christian message. Even theology is succumbing to the age of the fad.

In bringing Christian teachings into conversation with opposing viewpoints, it is important to understand that a Christian does not first solve every intellectual objection to Christian faith and then decide to believe. Christian faith is more than an intellectual decision, as I shall have occasion to note more than once in the pages that follow. One can even speak of the *unimportance* of theology in its preoccupation with words rather than the hard decisions involved in the commitment of faith. At the same time, coming to grips with theology is imperative for anyone who is serious about the meaning of that faith. The fact that the Christian message does constitute a formidable intellectual offense is further reason for one to consider it carefully. There is nothing rationally compelling, to say the least, about the claim that Jesus Christ is the definitive Word of God to humankind. On the contrary, there are many reasons to doubt the validity of this claim. Thus a book of this kind is not intended to prove or demonstrate the truth of Christian faith, and it is certainly not intended to make that faith more palatable at the expense of its own integrity. Its purpose rather is to clear away possible misunderstandings that can present unnecessary obstacles to its serious consideration, and to convey some of the power and profundity of the Christian message. It is indeed a message that speaks to the head, but if it does not speak to the total person— the heart as well as the head—then it will not likely *address* a person the way it is intended. One is not argued into Christian faith. One can only be invited.

Because this book is written for the non-theologian rather than the scholar, footnotes have been kept to a minimum. Those who have some theological background will recognize the influence of various theologians of our time, to whom I shall occasionally refer.

Besides the many from whom I have learned and whose work contribute to my own theological stance, there are those who have assisted me in very concrete ways in the preparation of this volume by reading various portions of it and offering their critique and suggestions. Among them I should mention two colleagues in the department of religion at Saint Xavier College, David Aune and Mary Lederer Roby, Steven Murphy who leads the Campus Ministry team at the college, and Pastor Dewey Bjorkman.

Having told my wife, Marilyn, of my intention to dedicate this modest undertaking to her, she replied that given the character of its content it would be more appropriate to dedicate it to our children. As usual, she was right. And so this book is dedicated to them, who with coming generations will face in their own time and circumstance the invitation to faith.

1

The Issue Is Faith

WHAT CAN I BELIEVE? This is a question which has always been asked, but perhaps never so dramatically as today. It is an important question because it is fundamental to the character of our lives. If we understand faith as that which expresses our basic commitments, hopes and aspirations, then faith is indeed a big word. It expresses what theologian Paul Tillich described as "ultimate concern," or the basic commitment in one's life which underlies and gives perspective to everything else. But what shall the content of that commitment be? This question is bothering many Christians today whose confidence in the religious tradition in which they have been raised has been shaken by the world in which they live. For many of them the words of Goethe express a truth in which they have become personally and often painfully involved: "The one most truly profound theme in the history of mankind, to which all other themes are subordinate, remains the struggle between unbelief and faith."

It is that struggle which has given rise to this book. Christian faith as the religious expression of the Western tradition is not something one can take for granted, like a piece of furniture that can never be moved. A considerable amount of literature has appeared in recent years, characterizing our times as a "post-Christian era" which is witnessing the steady demise of Christianity. Anyone who seeks to present the basic tenets of Christian faith today cannot do so without taking this claim seriously, spelling out for the reader the attraction and power of that faith—even today. This first chapter will accordingly be devoted to a discussion of the nature of Christian faith, some of the challenges to that faith that many are experiencing today, and the grounds on which the venture of faith is taken.

Religious Belief and Christian Faith

A familiar personality image in our culture, often conveyed over television, is that of the person who exudes an air of calm superiority and appears to have things well under control. "Playing it cool" expresses an ideal for many young people, who admire the air of detachment and the individual freedom of the person who does not let himself become involved. But as an attitude towards life, "playing it cool" falls short. If we try to avoid committing ourselves to ideals or causes which transcend ourselves, we end up with a self-centered life which helps no one, least of all ourselves. The real meaning of life consists of the commitments we are willing to make, the values we uphold, the goals to which we give ourselves. It is our commitments that define us or reveal us for what we are to other people. They are far more important than other ways in which people often seek to define us, whether in terms of our work, economic status, political party, or the color of our skin.

At the root of our values and commitments we all have certain fundamental convictions which provide some meaning to the world in which we live. Perhaps most of us do not reflect very much about those convictions. They operate as assumptions which are taken for granted and are not carefully analyzed, providing the setting in which we live and understand ourselves. Oftentimes (but not necessarily!) the more educated we become the more likely we are prodded into thinking critically about these assumptions. Or perhaps a crucial experience—a tragedy or some momentous event in our life—moves us to think about them and to find that our orientation toward life may be changing. These convictions are not purely theoretical but are built into our values and attitudes, providing a rationale for our understanding of what life is all about.

This aspect of our experience is an important part of what it means to be human. Presumably cows, dogs and even dolphins are not moved to act on the basis of deeply held convictions concerning life and its meaning. But for the human being, the experience of life brings forth this kind of response. We want to "see things clear and see them whole." We need to make sense out of life, to see some purpose and coherence in the total picture. Thus there are certain basic convictions which, if we are questioned long enough, we finally fall back on as the reason for our being and doing. They are not convictions which are necessarily obvious; they cannot be proven to the satisfaction of everyone who questions us; we may at times harbor some doubts about their truth ourselves. They are expressed as beliefs, or convictions which express our own personal creed.

These convictions might not be regarded as religious beliefs if they do not involve faith in God or if they do not find expression in organized worship. Yet one can argue that any affirmation concerning what life is all about is religious, because it expresses a faith which can be neither proved nor disproved. The belief, for example, that life is meaningful and not ultimately absurd may be based on grounds other than faith in God, but it is nonetheless faith in *something* which expresses an ultimate kind of commitment not subject to proof. One may decide that God does not exist and instead put one's trust in the inherent goodness of humankind, or in the ultimate power of love or justice, or in the power and absolute value of one's nation, or in capitalism or Communism as the answer to all human problems. Whatever becomes the source of meaning and sense for one's life becomes one's "god" in which one trusts. It provides a sense of identity for oneself and an orientation for value judgments, a function which faith in its customary religious expression has always provided.

The character of our present age can certainly be described as secular or "this-world-centered," yet I have been arguing that ultimate (religious) sorts of belief are to be found all around us. The ambiguities and uncertainties of life make believers of us all, whatever the beliefs may be. We seek an integrated and meaningful life and that involves some kind of faith, whether or not we call it religious. What we have witnessed during the nineteenth and twentieth centuries is a profound erosion of religious belief as it is customarily understood. Even the widespread notion that human beings are inherently religious *(homo religiosus)* has been challenged by those who see in our secular age a gradual disappearance of traditional belief in God. The ideas of Dietrich Bonhoeffer, a German theologian executed by the Nazis in 1945, have been particularly influential in making this point. In letters that he wrote from prison, Bonhoeffer suggested that we are "coming of age" in a technological world. We have become masters of our environment and no longer look to God for answers or solutions to human problems. We are no longer interested in the big questions concerning human destiny which philosophy and theology have perennially discussed, but are intent on solving the more immediate problems of life which can be addressed by our science and technology. Many theologians took Bonhoeffer and applied him to the crisis in religious belief that they perceived in their own time. Some concluded that our society had become so secularized that the notion of God no longer carried any meaning and that the vast majority of people now regarded religion as irrelevant. The religious person was disappearing.

The renewed interest in religion which has characterized the present decade has forced many people to reexamine these ideas. The secular spirit has not extinguished the serious religious questions which emerge from our experience of life—the questions of meaning and destiny. Bonhoeffer's importance is not in telling us that religion is dead, but in providing a critique of religion from the vantage point of Christian faith. Though his critique is invaluable, it is also overdrawn in that it places religion in diametrical opposition to Christian faith and fails to see the common features of both. The fact that religion has been present in the experience of every human community, and that questions of meaning and destiny surface wherever people have thought reflectively about themselves, is certainly significant to understanding what Christian faith is all about. Christians also seek a meaning and integration to life and their faith is essential to that quest.

Yet the critique of religion by Bonhoeffer and his teacher, the Swiss theologian Karl Barth, makes a valid point. These men were sensitive to the fact that we can use religion in selfish ways. The God of religious people can be an object of manipulation, or someone with whom they barter for their own advantage. One's use of prayer can reflect this, whenever God is summoned like a fireman to quickly extinguish one's troubles. Bonhoeffer's point is that *we* are in charge here; we are responsible for our world and cannot expect God to bail us out. The God of religion who does bail us out is no longer present, and Bonhoeffer argues that *that* God is not the God of Christian faith anyway. The Christian God is known in the life of Jesus Christ, and his power is the power of the cross, or suffering love.

But this point does not deny that Christianity as well as religion in general is concerned with answers to human problems. It provides consolation in the face of life's difficulties and inspiration to overcome them. It provides spiritual resources for living one's life. The importance of these resources is difficult to deny. But at the same time, Christian faith *is* different from other religious faiths simply because of the distinctive content of its faith. That content will be discussed later; we simply note here that the distinctiveness of Christian faith is rooted in the figure of Jesus Christ. To say this is to recognize, among other things, that ideas concerning God do not descend full-blown from heaven. They are rooted in the historical experience of a people and expressed in their traditions. The Christian faith is shaped by the peculiar experience of the people of Israel, the Jews, out of whose history emerged Jesus of Nazareth. Jesus dealt creatively with the tradition of his people, and in his life—his teaching, his ministry, his death and the remarkable events that followed his death—Christians perceive a revelation of who God is and what life is intended to be. The distinctiveness of Christianity as a religion, then, is based on the distinctiveness of the historical object of its faith, Jesus Christ, and the picture of God that his life conveys. In subsequent chapters we shall expand on the implications of faith in Christ; at this point we want to present its meaning in very broad and simple strokes.

The message concerning Jesus that has been told through the centuries is called Gospel, or "good news." That term interprets the meaning of Jesus' life and provides the basis for understanding the distinctive nature of Christian faith. It is a response to the good news that the final word concerning life is not only that "God is," but that "God is love." This is no obvious truth, for there is much in life which would lead us to despair. The fear and hatred which divide and alienate people too often rule human relationships and make people cynical about the possibility of a truly self-giving love. But Jesus' life tells the Christian that love is stronger than hate, and in the midst of the distorted relationships of life the power of love can reconcile and make all things new. Jesus and his cross portray the power of suffering love and express that love as the final word concerning human life and destiny.

Christian faith is also a resurrection faith because the fate of Jesus was not sealed by the grave; he was "raised from the dead." This tells the Christian that the final word is not death, but life. Not only hate, but even death can be transformed into new life. The mystery of Jesus' resurrection now overshadows the mystery of death, proclaiming a message of joy and hope in the face of this ultimate enemy. In a purely biological sense, of course, death is simply the natural conclusion of life. Death by natural causes at the end of a full life can even be welcomed. But this does not deny the threat inherent to death. We are more than biological organisms and one is not inclined to face one's *own* death as a simply natural event. The very question of life's meaning and destiny in the face of death compels us to raise the question of life beyond death. Christian faith, in hearing the resurrection story, affirms that God is sovereign over our death as well as our life.

Because the Gospel is a story of divine love and victory over death, it elicits a faith marked by gratitude and thanksgiving. Christian faith is a response to what it perceives God has done in the story of Jesus, both as a historical event some 2000 years ago and as an event which is happening in the lives of people today. An anchor has been established in the Gospel which provides a new perspective on life, inspiring gratitude and confidence even in the face of those powers which would threaten to destroy meaningful life and community. This means that faith is at the same time the profound expression of hope. It holds forth the vision of what life can and will be, if not in this age, then in the next. Christian faith looks forward to a final transformation in which "all things shall become new," and that vision inspires confidence rather than despair.

It should be clear by now that the possibility of Christian faith is not simply the possibility of believing that something is true. To be sure, there is a distinctive content to Christian faith which involves both history and interpretation of that history, but the point is that this content inspires a response which involves the whole person. Faith is not simply an intellectual decision (though it is also that); it is being "captured" by the Gospel and responding with one's whole being to a message that excites gratitude and hope. Faith can best be described in terms of commitment or discipleship. It is being turned around in order to set off on a new path in which one's life is governed by a new vision and new priorities. The commitment embodied in this faith expresses a trusting relationship to God, whose will and purpose is seen by the Christian in the life and ministry of Jesus. Faith, then, is putting your life on the line, commiting yourself, recognizing Jesus as Lord because his life expresses God's purpose for you.

How does one come to such a faith? Christians generally would say (and those within the Reformation tradition would say it with particular emphasis) that faith is a gift, which means they are aware that faith is not something which they have generated or produced within themselves. Faith is no achievement of their own, nothing about which they could boast. On the contrary, faith arises when I am addressed by the Gospel in such a way that the message illumines my life, revealing myself to myself through the words of that story. It involves a double-take, in which I become aware of myself in a new way: I am in the presence of God, and it is Jesus who has brought me there. I now see myself as I had not seen myself before.

This experience does not occur through any magic formula; no particular procedure makes it automatic. There is of course an inherent power in the story of Jesus—in his exalted teachings of God's love and the invitation to put one's trust in his heavenly Father, in his own selflessness and sense of mission which brought him finally to the cross, in his compassionate and forgiving spirit. But the story of Jesus first takes on religious significance for me when I see that story in relation to my own needs and goals and vulnerabilities as a human being. As the message of good news, it is not until I hear that message speaking to *me* that faith becomes a possibility. At that point the message challenges me to decision. It forces upon me a moment of truth which I may seek either to avoid or to respond to in an act of acceptance or rejection.

We noted in the opening paragraphs of this chapter that faith of one kind or another is not an option but a necessity. Life is mystery and life is often problematic, forcing us to reach out for answers which cannot be rationally demonstrated but can only be affirmed in an act of faith. During the course of our lives we arrive at certain beliefs concerning the "big questions" that life poses for us: Who am I? Is there a God? What does it mean to me? How can I gain self-fulfillment? What is our destiny as human beings? These questions are answered in the character and direction of our lives, the commitments, ideals and aspirations which define us to ourselves and to others. Thus the possibility of Christian faith is not a matter of believing something instead of nothing, but of committing oneself to the Christian vision of God and human life instead of some other vision. We turn now to consider some of the problems that raise serious questions in the minds of Christians and others concerning the truth of Christian belief.

Challenges to Christian Faith

There has never been a time when Christians have not encountered skeptical attitudes concerning the content of their belief. There is certainly sufficient reason to think, however, that our own times bring particularly powerful challenges to its credibility. These challenges can be regarded as intellectual in nature in the sense that they arise from an inquiring intellect, but they are not purely intellectual problems. Christian faith, as we have noted, is more than giving an intellectual assent to the truth of particular statements about reality. It is an expression of one's whole life to the question, "What is life all about?" and therefore the challenges to that faith arise from the whole gamut of life-experiences. I shall consider a few of those challenges which I find to be particularly significant, and indicate a possible response to each of them. These remarks will have to be brief but perhaps they can at least indicate the direction in which many Christians would respond.

Faith in a "Post-Christian Era"

There are many signs in our contemporary society which point to an erosion of religious belief. We have noted that people are inherently religious in the sense that they seek a commitment which gives meaning to themselves and to their world. Yet traditional religious beliefs which have been shaped by the Christian tradition appear to be weakening. Sociologists of religion report that even among church members there is a growing tendency either to question the doctrines of the church or to suspend one's judgment on them. There is a certain weariness with institutional religion and the traditional orthodoxies, while at the same time the quest for answers to the mystery of life remains as intense as ever. In our society relatively few people say they are atheists, and yet when questioned they often have serious reservations about belief in a personal God who answers prayer. College students in religion courses often express disillusionment with the traditional theism of the church, in which God is pictured as a larger-than-life human being who resides in a heavenly realm upstairs. The crisis in traditional Christianity is certainly intertwined with the doubts people have concerning the Christian doctrine of God.

During the sixties a number of theologians created considerable excitement even in the secular press when they asserted that "God is dead." There were various meanings to this statement, but a dominant one was the contention that the God of traditional Christian belief is no longer a reality for the secular society that had emerged in our time. As one theologian put it, "The man in tune with our culture does not believe in God." These impressions have occasioned numerous prophecies concerning the eventual extinction of Christianity. Those who speak of the post-Christian era usually mean that the 2000-year history of the Christian tradition has now come to the end of its predominant position in the Western world, but it is still too early to discern what kind of religious expression will take its place.

The proliferation of religious cults in our own time is seen by many as another symptom of Christianity's death. We are witnessing a wide array of religious and semi-religious movements, actively competing for our allegiance and offering every conceivable panacea for the human spirit. Their presence indicates that many people no longer regard Christianity as a viable commitment and are looking for something else. The interest of Americans in Eastern religions has been particularly significant. A staggering variety of cults and gurus have invited the restless American to new levels of consciousness and self-fulfillment through the art of contemplation. In most of these movements, the vast majority of the adherents are young people who have been alienated from the religious traditions of their family and society.

Further evidence of discontent with traditional Christianity is the emergence of numerous sects on the fringe of the church, characterized by an intense experiential religion. Charismatic groups stress the gifts of the Spirit, including faith-healing and speaking in tongues. They claim a certainty of faith and a "joy in the Spirit" which they do not find in the fellowship of typical church members. We must look more closely at this phenomenon in our discussion of the Holy Spirit; at this point we simply note some ecclesiastical and cultural implications of the massive increase in spirit-movements within the mainline churches. These groups have often been seen as defensive expressions against the erosions of Christian belief, with their claim to an intense and unusual experience of the presence of God. It is an immediate and overpowering experience which apparently leaves no room for doubt, just at a time when the credibility of Christian faith is being widely assaulted.

History amply demonstrates that periods of turmoil and stress will turn people inward to find some rock-bottom guarantee of the religious truth they profess, and thus this kind of religious expression in our own time is understandable. On the other hand, it is quite possible that these movements may make an important contribution in shaping the church which is to come. To analyze them from a purely sociological or psychological perspective is inadequate in portraying their significance to the Christian faith-community. The extent of whatever positive impact they may have remains to be seen.

It is threatening to Christians to reflect on the possibility of Christianity gradually disappearing. It is threatening to their understanding of the Gospel which they regard as God's Word to the human race. It is threatening to their understanding of Jesus' promise that the church will prevail against the powers of death (Matt. 16:18). But when one takes the long view and asks, "What will it be like in the year 5,000 or 10,000 A.D.?" (should there be any point in looking that far ahead!) then one may well wonder what will remain from life today as we know it. There is nothing that escapes the ravages of time; will Christianity also move from its beginnings to its maturity and then to its old age and death? At this point Christians can only affirm their conviction that as long as human beings retain their identity as mortal creatures who must live by faith, the Gospel of Jesus Christ will continue to be a light along the way. The institutional forms of Christianity will change—must change—in order to minister effectively and communicate its message in changing times, but I trust that the Gospel itself is too great a gift to be lost.

There is always a tension between church and society, and in an age when the church's message is increasingly disregarded and even consigned to the junk-heap of outmoded ideas, Christians must be reminded of St. Paul's words that the Gospel of Christ is "folly" to the wisdom of the age (1 Cor. 1:18ff.). At the same time, Christians cannot afford to withdraw from meaningful involvement in and communication with their society. The Gospel is not addressed to a religious few but to the world, and the church is responsible for communicating that Gospel as effectively as it can whatever the cultural milieu. This means that conventional forms of Christianity must be continually rethought and reformed. Christians must realize (if they do not already) that they can no longer assume that they are living in a Christian nation. We are living in a pluralistic society in which the preeminence of the Christian religion can no longer be taken for granted. A common assumption of our times is that all starting points are equally valid, and no one religion has a monopoly on the truth. Christians are now often reminded that the viability of their faith cannot be judged by how many of their neighbors share it. They have never been a majority in this world and have no reason to think they ever will be.

The mind-set of a secular society is a constant challenge to Christian consciousness. We are inevitably influenced by the culture in which we live, but the prevailing ideas and assumptions of any particular age should never be considered absolute. Some times and places will provide a more hospitable environment for Christian faith, but this is not an unmixed blessing. Christians cannot expect to be fully at home in any cultural environment, and history tells us that the more hostile a society is to Christian faith, the more vital that faith is. Whatever the changing times bring, there remains the conviction that the God who is "Father of our Lord Jesus Christ" is Lord of history itself. This does not mean that God is pulling the strings, but it does mean that the Christian looks to the future with hope. The post-Christian era may signify change that threatens our image of the church and its place in society, but to Christian faith it is simply a challenge to a more creative response to the opportunities of our time.

Faith and Relativism

Sociologists and anthropologists have made us aware of the relativity of our knowledge. We have often been forced to modify our ideas about "universal truths" after getting acquainted with the traditions of other peoples living in quite different cultural environments. We are impressed by the fact that our views of life and human destiny are intertwined with our own history, and what we see is dependent on where we are standing. When we make our own viewpoints absolute, we are in effect judging the traditions of others by our own, a practice which any college student is quick to recognize as ethnocentric. On the college campus today the opposite viewpoint is clearly in command; the fundamental truth appears to be that there are no fundamental or universal truths that are valid for all people.

This perspective has had great impact on people's attitudes toward religion, and Christianity in particular. Christian faith has always proclaimed Jesus Christ as a universal Word of God, a message for all people and for all times. The impact of relativism, on the other hand, has encouraged Christians to turn their faith into a private possession which is "right" for them but not necessarily for their neighbor. Religion has become a matter of taste; you either like it or you don't. Since there is no generally recognized way of determining the truth or falsity of beliefs concerning God and human destiny, the alternative seems attractive to remove religious beliefs from the realm of objective truth, and make them judgments of emotion or personal preference. They then have no reference to a reality which is independent of themselves, but simply express their own subjectivity. The final conclusion to this process is the vacuous statement, "It makes no difference what you believe, just so long as you're sincere!"

Christians must recognize the danger of this kind of thinking. While it is true that Christianity is not simply a list of statements about reality, it is certainly a commitment that affirms the reality of God as we know him in Jesus Christ. This means that statements of *cognitive* value are being made about God and his relationship to human beings, even though such statements are not subject to mathematical or empirical proof.[1] The nature of faith is to affirm a truth that can only be *affirmed* and not demonstrated. In an age that exalts scientific knowledge as the epitome of truth and certainty, it is not surprising that religious affirmations concerning reality are denied all cognitive value. Today we are witnessing a reaction to the mentality generated by a scientific world view, and the richness of human experience, including the religious, is more apt to be appreciated. Yet the actual truth-value of religious statements remains suspect; religion is simply a reflection of one's personal convictions and their worth is dependent on how well they work or provide satisfaction to the individual. Relativism thus reflects a lack of confidence in the possibility of any knowledge of God, which results in each person possessing his own truth or his own god.

This kind of thinking is challenged by Christian experience, in which one is addressed by the Gospel message and persuaded of its truth. The message of the good news illumines the Christian's life and gives it an orientation from which the rest of life can be understood. If the Gospel is not the truth for human life, then that truth must be found somewhere else. What one lives by may be a choice of convenience for some, but not for the Christian. The truth captures people rather than people capturing their own particular truth. This does not mean that there is no *relativity* to our knowledge of God. Relativity is inevitable in the sense that we are all located in space and time and our views on life and destiny reflect that location, but this does not deny the general meaningfulness or truth of our knowledge of God as is implied in relativism. Obviously there are different perceptions of God that are rooted in the various religious traditions of the world. These perceptions can be seen as complementary to each other, but they may also contradict each other and necessitate rejection if we are true to the image of God we have come to know. Thus Christian faith affirms the possibility of our knowledge of God and consequently rejects relativism as a loss of confidence in that possibility.

Faith and Self-deception

How do we know that faith in God is not self-deception? Could not God be a construct of our own needs as human beings, a figment of the imagination which we project "out there" but who is *not* out there? This question was raised most forcefully among theologians in the nineteenth century by Ludwig Feuerbach. He maintained that our ideas of God, heaven and eternal life are projections of human needs and desires and cannot be given any credibility. Theology is anthropology, the expression of human aspirations; it tells us about ourselves, not God.

Sigmund Freud provided support for these ideas in his development of psychoanalysis. He maintains in *The Future of an Illusion* that religion is derived from the helplessness experienced by infants and children. The notion of God expresses the authority and comfort which the child finds in his father. Religious people attempt to satisfy infantile needs when they project the father-image onto a "God" who is all-powerful, all-knowing and compassionate. Religion as well as art, says Freud, provides an escape from the grim realities of life. But where art is recognized as illusion, religion is not. Thus religion can be regarded as a delusion of the masses, providing a distorted view of reality and preventing people from growing up and facing the real world in a mature way. Religious faith is self-deception.

For many people this psychological critique of religion is the one that gives them the most serious doubts about the validity of faith. How does the Christian respond to this critique? Obviously there must be something about the experience of faith that stands up against the charge that it is illusory or simply wish-fulfillment. Yet people who believe cannot provide a definitive proof for the truth of their faith-commitment to one who does not share it. Reasons can be given to make sense out of Christian faith, but the validity of that faith is not known except as one participates in it. This is necessarily so as long as one maintains that Christian faith always involves the establishing of a relationship of trust to Jesus Christ, whose life for the Christian constitutes a revelation of God.

Freud's critique of faith reveals a fundamentally different view of what is ultimately real. His critique is based on an opposite faith which also cannot be proved: there is no God. But beyond this, there are some questions one can raise about his argument. The idea that religion is a mark of immaturity would imply that irreligion is a mark of maturity, but it would likely be difficult to make either case. Moreover, the insights of psychoanalysis can be directed just as well at those concerned to attack religion. Perhaps the hostility toward God is the misdirected hostility toward one's father, or an atheistic world view is one's reaction to the hated symbols of authority. None of this proves the reality or unreality of the object of religious belief, however.

Sometimes Christians have tried to refute the psychological critique of religion by attempting to isolate faith from the psychology of belief, defining faith as unique, a divine gift which is not subject to psychological analysis. Yet every experience is psychological and subject to analysis. To speak of faith as gift is a theological judgment and does not deny the psychological (or any other) factors at work in the emergence of faith. In this chapter we have been speaking of faith within the context of the human quest for meaning and hope, amid the realities of evil and death. Faith never occurs in a vacuum.

We cannot leave this critique of faith without noting that there is something very important to learn from it. Freud sees religion functioning as a security blanket, and he is critical of the way he sees religious people using God to guarantee their own security. Karl Marx sees religion functioning in a similar way when he condemns it as an "opiate of the people." We cannot afford to miss the validity of these judgments. Religion is too often my attempt to manipulate God, to assure myself that "somebody up there likes me." Religion is expected to guarantee a solicitous God who will take care of me if I pay him sufficient attention and obey the Ten Commandments. What men and women of biblical faith have perceived over against this kind of religion (at least since the Old Testament prophets) is that God is sovereign and not subject to human manipulation. He is not an omnipotent servant at our disposal but the Lord of life who calls us to account. In other words, Christian faith is not a faith of consolation without at the same time being a faith which exposes us to the shattering judgment of God, who makes us aware of our weaknesses and calls us to a life of faithfulness. Such a God is not the selfish creation of any human being, but the God who speaks to us in the life of Jesus Christ.

Faith and Human Tragedy

Perhaps the challenge to Christian faith that is most difficult in a personal or existential sense is the immense tragedy of life that threatens any sense of meaningfulness or purpose in the human story. This is the challenge of evil that has always posed a theological problem for Christians. How could a good God create a world in which evil prevails? Perhaps this way of putting the question is overly pessimistic, and yet there are the singular tragedies in our history which defy any attempt to understand them or harmonize them with a divine purpose. The event which has practically come to symbolize this problem for the twentieth century is the Holocaust, Hitler's attempt to exterminate the Jews. Can one reconcile that event with faith in the God of Abraham, Isaac, and Jacob? Richard Rubenstein, the author of *After Auschwitz,* concludes that the biblical faith is no longer viable because the God of the Jews is dead.

The writer who has perhaps most forcefully confronted Christians with this problem in recent times is Albert Camus. His book,

The Plague, is a powerful treatment of the absurdity of human suffering in which he rejects the possibility of a Christian answer. As a child slowly dies an excruciating death, the priest affirms that even this can be accepted in spite of our inability to understand. But the doctor replies that he cannot accept a scheme of things in which children are tortured like this. In *The Myth of Sisyphus,* Camus challenges us to face the ultimate absurdity of life, recognizing that there is no rationality or meaning to be found to this puzzling universe. We may be able to make sense out of many things *within* our world, but the kinds of questions asked by human beings as to purpose and ultimate destiny are met by an overpowering silence. The absurdity of the human condition is that we have needs which our world cannot fulfill. One possible answer to this situation is suicide, which Camus seriously considers, but he concludes that the most heroic response we can make is to affirm the value of human life even in the face of absurdity.

Many people become impatient with the literature of existentialist authors, like Camus, who they believe are preoccupied with negative thoughts and are too one-sided to be taken seriously. Yet the Christian cannot dismiss these authors for they have identified the crucial question which stands behind the restlessness of human life: the question of the meaningfulness of our lives which are threatened by a sense of the loss of God, by suffering, tragedy, and ultimately death. There is no simple answer which Christians can give to this question. There is no rational solution which will remove the painful ambiguities of human life. Yet the Gospel of Jesus Christ speaks directly and powerfully to these ambiguities.

Christians do not believe in a God who is behind the scenes, pulling the strings on all that happens. The life of Jesus Christ has become the defining center for our understanding of God, which means that God is present to us precisely *in* the tragedy and suffering of life. To consider Jesus is to consider the cross and the power of suffering love. It identifies the power of God with the weakness of human beings as they confront a threatening and overpowering universe. Death is a pervading, disconcerting presence in human life; death in a thousand ways, crushing the human spirit and bringing to destruction all that we value. The power of evil always seems to overcome the more fragile power of life and the potential for good in the human spirit. But the message of the cross is a message of life in the face of death, of victory in the face of defeat, for out of death comes resurrection!

Thus the Christian response to the tragic and absurd in human life is not an intellectual answer which could explain *why* things are the way they are. It is rather an invitation to believe, i.e., to trust that the life, death, and resurrection of Jesus does provide the clue to life's meaning. It is an invitation to trust in the God whom Jesus called "Father," believing that the disparate threads of meaninglessness will finally weave something that is meaningful; that the power of love is ultimately greater than evil; that out of death will come new life. It is a faith that is constantly assaulted, yet one that is constantly nurtured by the Gospel, that story in the midst of our human history that expresses the ultimate sovereignty of divine love. The beauty and power of that story helps Christians to put things in order as they look at the human scene, not in the sense that they now have all the answers, but in the sense that they now live in the hope inspired by that story.

In considering these challenges to their faith, it is well for Christians to be reminded of a distinction made by Martin Luther concerning the nature of faith. He noted that there is a *certainty* inherent to faith inspired by the Gospel of Christ, but that this certainty is not *security*. By this he meant that Christians are always "on the way" and never arrive; they never get beyond the doubts and obstacles which make the life of faith a pilgrimage and adventure. There is no such thing as absolute certainty or security in this life, and we cannot expect it. There is inspiration and hope, consolation and joy in the life of one who believes but there is also the frequent afflictions of doubt, turmoil and confusion. For the Christian to expect security is to deny the mercies of God as well as the realities of existence. It is to forget, as well, that security invites self-righteousness, the particular enemy of the religious person. The only way one can live is on the basis of faith, and the Gospel of Christ provides that basis in the midst of the ambiguities and challenges of life.

In this chapter we have considered some challenges to Christian faith as a prelude to consideration of the actual content of that faith. In the chapters that follow we shall spell out that content, being particularly attentive to certain misunderstandings which place unnecessary obstacles before the inquiring person. Now and then we shall refer to the problems we have just discussed, for they are an important part of the cultural milieu in which Christians live out their faith. But our primary purpose is to present the fundamental tenets of Christian belief so that the reader understands the basis of the Christian commitment. In carrying out this task, we hope to resist the temptation to minimize in any way that challenge which confronts us at the very center of Christian faith: Jesus Christ himself, and his call to discipleship.

2

Faith and Theology

WE BEGAN THE PRECEDING CHAPTER with a discussion of faith, noting that human beings live by some kind of faith which expresses the meaning of things as they see it, and embodies their hopes and aspirations. We then discussed the distinctive characteristics of Christian faith and the various challenges to that faith which the Christian encounters in today's world. In doing this we have been reflecting on what Christian faith is all about and how it relates to our particular cultural environment. In a nutshell, this is what theology is. We might define Christian theology as reflection on what Christians believe, within the context of their particular world. Theology is a natural expression of faith, for it expresses the need to understand the implications of one's faith-commitment. "Doing theology" helps Christians to clarify their faith in view of the contemporary experience of their Christian community and the historic teachings of the church, and in view of other commitments and views of life that are found in their society.

Like every academic discipline, theology makes use of methods which are appropriate to the study of its subject-matter. In this chapter we shall consider some of the concepts that are important to theological reflection, such as authority, the role of scripture and tradition, the concept of revelation, and its implications in relating Christianity to other religions of the world. It is important to note that theology should be distinguished from those approaches to religion which are governed by the methods of other disciplines, such as philosophy of religion, psychology of religion, and sociology of religion. These other disciplines do not presuppose faith, nor even necessarily any personal involvement with faith which would at least recognize its importance and integrity. Students of these disciplines seek to study religion "from a distance," regarding it as a phenomenon to be observed and analyzed on the basis of the assumptions of their discipline. At the same time, while theologians are "insiders," they are not unrelated to those who stand outside their circle of belief. They are concerned to relate that belief in all of its implications to the total world of human life with its various commitments. This means they are open to dialogue with those who are students of religion but who may not share their commitment of faith.

The Theologian's Task

One can identify two poles in the understanding of theology as we have described it: the past, consisting of the Christian tradition going back to the biblical record and interpreted by the church through the ages, and the present in the form of the culture in which the theologian is working and which provides the setting and challenge for interpreting the Christian message here and now. This means that theology, contrary to the impression some theologians may give, should never simply be repetition of ancient truths or removed from the concrete issues of contemporary life. Theology involves not only the need to listen attentively to Christian tradition, but also the important constructive task of interpreting the Christian message for today. In fulfilling this task, theology is not an end in itself but a servant of the faith-community. It should help Christians to mold their attitudes and actions in responsible Christian living. The theologians who do their work well are those who are well rooted in the Christian tradition and identify themselves with it, and at the same time are perceptive students of their own times who can creatively relate and interpret the Gospel in terms of the language and thinking of their contemporaries. One can discern in this work both a *conserving* and a *creative* task, conserving the essential message of the church and creatively interpreting it for today.

Many Christians have difficulty in appreciating the need of creative theologizing. They can understand the need to conserve and pass on the doctrines of the church, but are unsettled by new theological interpretations or unfamiliar theological language and are prone to shout "heresy!" when they encounter it. These people do not understand the historically conditioned character of human thinking, including our ideas about God and what is ultimately real, about the human condition, and about the universe in which we live. It involves the problem of relativity in our thinking and the fact that the Christian tradition stretches over two millennia. During this time many profound changes have taken place in the way in which people have understood themselves and their world. To use a common and quite fundamental example, the ancient person perceived a three-tiered universe of heaven, earth and hell, and naturally the Christian understanding of God and the story of salvation were understood within this conceptual framework.

With the rise of science and the secularization of Western society, this three-fold view of reality has lost its credibility; for many centuries it was taken for granted, but for some time now this has no longer been the case. Theologians today are compelled to interpret the meaning of the Gospel in a "thought-world" or "life-world" which reflects our own time rather than that of ancient or medieval people. Yet of course the continuities remain for we are still in the midst of the human story. We remain mortal beings, caught in the mystery of what it means to be human, doing battle with our all-too-human weaknesses, anxious about the unknown, and chafing over the limitations which life imposes upon us. But to communicate the Gospel in a way that makes it count, the ancient dogmas cannot simply be repeated. They beg for new language in order that the message may be heard.

These two poles of past and present point us to two prevailing orientations in carrying out the theological task: conservative and liberal. One might question the usefulness of these terms because they have become identified with stereotyped positions. Often one is conservative or liberal as a matter of temperament or as an ideological stance which results in predictable responses, whether one is discussing politics, economics, or religion. But my use of these terms is to denote a viewpoint which comes *as a result* of considering the dimensions of a particular theological issue. That consideration will lead one to be primarily concerned to reconcile one's position on the issue with the church's tradition (conservative), or to be primarily concerned to find a suitable position for today, even if it appears to be a departure from the tradition (liberal). One can see that both orientations have their proper validity, for on the one hand there is something to be conserved and communicated in Christian theology, while on the other hand the historically conditioned character of the church's message demands continuing effort to give it a contemporary expression.

The weakness of people who tend to think conservatively is that their concern with the tradition can prevent them from living fully in the present and responding creatively to their times. They may be guilty of exalting the theological insights of a previous generation or even of a previous century without appreciating the need for a more contemporary expression of the Gospel.

The weakness of those who take the liberal position is that their concern to be relevant may justify an uncritical acceptance of their culture's thought-world, leading them to impose an interpretation upon the church's message which seriously compromises the historically understood intention of that message. Theologians, just like everyone else, are children of their times, but the tradition in which they stand as Christians should give them some distance and perspective in evaluating the prevailing world views and values of their culture.

Because of its pervasive influence among large numbers of American Christians, it may be appropriate to note here a particular theological stance which is often characterized as a right-wing expression of conservative Christianity. It is fundamentalism, which took definite shape as a movement of reaction to liberal or modernist theologies at the beginning of the twentieth century. There had been considerable reunderstanding and adaptation of Christian belief in nineteenth century Protestant liberalism, but modernism described a yet more radical approach which used a scientific world view to judge the validity of religious faith. Christianity became little more than a vague belief in a supreme being, and the notion of revelation associated with the scriptures was rejected.

Fundamentalists perceived the essential problem to be the status

of the Bible. Was it really the Word of God or wasn't it? In order
to safeguard the Bible from the work of scholars who appeared to
be questioning all the traditional understandings of the biblical
material,[1] fundamentalists asserted that because the Bible was inspired it was absolutely free of any kind of error. It was a radical
defensive measure intended to secure such teachings as the substitu-
tionary death of Jesus Christ, his virgin birth, the resurrection, and
the second coming as a physical reappearance of Jesus. The inerrancy of scripture is the hallmark of fundamentalist belief. It distinguishes them from conservative Christians who would sympa-
thize with their concern to maintain the fundamental Christian
teachings but who regard the inerrancy of scripture as both a mistaken view of divine inspiration and an irresponsible view of the
Bible in light of our knowledge today. Another prominent feature
of fundamentalism has been its suspicion of any attempt to relate
the church's message to society at large. Attention is exclusively
focused upon the individual and the question of his personal salvation.[2]

The challenge inherent to interpreting the Christian tradition
which stretches back to ancient times is of course heightened now
by the post-Christian mentality which pervades much of our Western culture. Theologians are particularly aware of the problems
involved in relating the traditional supernaturalism of Christian
theology to a world which finds such thinking archaic. Their own
theological positions will often make it difficult for them to communicate genuinely to most Christian laypeople and even large
numbers of the clergy, whose theology is often uncritical and liter-
alistic. This is a burden to theologians and a cause of suspicion and
general uneasiness among the laity and ecclesiastical leadership. By
the very nature of their work, theologians are actually in the middle
of two competing moralities. On the one hand they are identified
with the Christian tradition and seek to affirm it and be loyal to it,
and on the other hand they are committed to an authentic study
of that tradition, with the assumption that their minds are open to
wherever the critical evidence leads them. Competent theologians
recognize this tension and are willing to live with it, but it may
prevent them from being as forthright or dogmatic about various

beliefs treasured by the tradition as their ecclesiastical superiors would like them to be!

I have referred several times to the Christian tradition, and this may have puzzled those who are more acutely aware of a plurality of traditions rather than one, monolithic tradition. It is of course true that there has been division within the Christian church so that we can in broad terms speak of three distinctive Christian traditions: the Latin or Roman Catholic, Eastern Orthodoxy, and Protestantism.[3] Theologians will reflect in their theological stance and method whether they come out of one or another of these traditions. Each bears a peculiar history, a peculiar context for its understanding of the Christian life, a peculiar worship system and a peculiar theology. The result of all this has been to isolate each tradition from the other. The divisions that occurred in the distant past have dominated the ecclesiastical scene, and when theologians addressed each other over the boundaries of their traditions it was invariably with the intent to refute each other.

Now however, one of the most significant developments in the life of the twentieth century church is the ecumenical movement, which was given tremendous impetus during the 1960s by the Second Vatican Council. It is the attempt on the part of churches to recognize and increasingly realize their unity under the lordship of Christ. One of the results of this movement (as well as furthering the movement along) has been the attempt on the part of theologians, particularly Roman Catholic and Protestant, to move out of a denominational orientation and to speak to each other and listen to each other in a spirit of understanding. Though there are distinctive traditions within the Christian heritage, there is nonetheless a common tradition we all share—"one lord, one faith, one baptism," as St. Paul expressed it—which provides a unity which is higher and deeper than any of the divisions that have emerged in the often tempestuous history of the church. It is the continuing task of theologians to celebrate and further that unity. Those theologians today who are at the forefront in shaping theological discussion are not narrowly oriented to their own traditions but are speaking to the whole Christian world.

There are other factors besides one's own religious tradition that

influence a person's theological stance. There are personal factors
involving personality traits, one's life history, and one's response
to the Christian message. There is the influence of philosophical
ideas and assumptions which provide the framework for a theologian's presentation of his theology. Today they may be existentialist categories or process philosophy or some other philosophical
heritage which provides a language and conceptual vehicle for expressing fundamental theological ideas. This is one way in which
theology fulfills that important part of its task to speak to its own
times in language and concepts which are familiar and meaningful.
Some would say that all theology must do is speak the language
of the Bible, but this raises the whole historical and cultural problem which we have noted above, which gets in the way of the
church's communicating the biblical message in our own time. It
is also naive to suppose we can jump back 2000 years without being influenced by the intervening centuries of Christian theology
which have shaped our own understanding of the biblical message.

The Question of Authority

There has always been tension in the church concerning the
exercise of authority in carrying out the theological task. The tension is the ever-present one between order and freedom. To be a
genuine community, the church must recognize the individual
integrity of those who carry on the work of theology, while at the
same time exercising an understandable concern to maintain a basic
continuity with the tradition. The message of "Fiddler on the
Roof" is indisputably true for the church as well as any other
group: one's tradition is essential to one's identity. The task is to
live the tradition in a spirit of freedom rather than to be bound
and stifled by it under a spirit of legalism or authoritarianism.

The presence of differing and even conflicting theological views
within the church often puzzles lay people. "If theologians of the
church can't agree among themselves," they ask, "then what is happening to the Christian faith and the Gospel we proclaim?" This
is a legitimate concern but it also reflects some confusion about the
nature of theology. It is helpful in addressing this problem if one

distinguishes between dogma, or the fundamental teachings of the church which are essential to the Gospel it proclaims, and doctrines which do not bear this fundamental character.

Dogma are those usually brief statements of belief hammered out in the early centuries at councils which involved the whole church and which really defined the essential content of the Christian faith—the dogmas of the Trinity and of Jesus Christ.[4] They do not repeat biblical language but express the church's perception of the basic teachings of scripture in the philosophical categories of the fourth and fifth centuries. They were shaped by the particular theological controversies of that time.

Doctrine is a wider category which would encompass all the teachings of the church and which vary in their relative importance to the Gospel message.

Theology is a broader term yet and refers to the whole range of reflection and inquiry carried on by religious thinkers. We have noted the various factors that enter into a person's theological position, and it is no surprise that there are differences from one theologian to another. Indeed, the test of the vitality of the church's theology is the extent to which there are differences in theological perspective and a genuine exchange between differing viewpoints. There can be essential unity in respect to dogma with significantly different theologies in terms of their organizing principles, conceptual framework and theological emphases. Today, as one might expect there is a plurality of theological "schools," reflecting the pluralistic world in which we live. Each has something to offer in enhancing Christian self-understanding and in helping the church to interpret its message. Church leadership should have the confidence that those theologies which most adequately carry out the theological task will predominate over those which may bear serious weaknesses. If this confidence is lost and the church seeks to restrict theological inquiry, then the freedom necessary to the task of theology is destroyed and the church itself is impoverished.

But what if a particular theologian attacks a dogma of the church? Must he not be excommunicated and his views repudiated by the church in an official, public act? This would be a serious problem, particularly if the theologian is engaged by the church in instructing its future pastors or priests. His ideas would properly be called heretical, because a dogma expresses such an essential truth that to dispute it literally pulls the rug out from under the Gospel. Yet it is also true that heresy trials and public excommunications are no ways for the church to exercise its authority. The church must honor the integrity of the individual in question and through its theologians address the issue with him in an effort to arrive at an understanding of what he is really saying. If it is clear that his position is so basically at variance with the essential message of the Gospel as to negate that message—to deny that Jesus is indeed the Word of God—then his own ministry as a theologian has been rejected and he is no longer a servant of the faith-community. But the church must listen attentively to him before passing judgment, because the history of theology has shown that heretics are often expressing in exaggerated form some truth within the tradition which was not being sufficiently recognized. A genuine heretic often serves an important function for the church, even if in a negative way.

When we turn from the exercise of authority to the source of authority in the practice of faith and theology, we find several well-defined answers. For Christianity as well as for most of the world's religions, a sacred scripture is central to the faith. The Bible is the source-document for the church's understanding of its message, containing eye-witness accounts of Jesus' ministry and the witness of the apostles (those who were sent out by the church to spread the Gospel). Protestant Christians make the Bible the explicit standard or authority for Christian faith and theology, which means that theology in every age must ultimately be judged in terms of its faithfulness to the message concerning Jesus Christ which the scriptures convey. Though Protestants make the Bible their authority, this does not mean they agree on all theological issues. The principal reason for this is that the theological meaning of biblical passages involves interpretation, and this interpretation always reflects the experience and theological concerns of the particular group that does the interpreting. The meaning they find in certain biblical passages may not be the intended meaning of the author, or the meaning another community of faith finds in it. Another factor in this problem is that already in the New Testament there are several different theological perspectives informing the material, and these differences will appear in the theological stance of the various church traditions. For example, the theology of the apostle Paul heavily influenced Martin Luther and the Protestant Reformation, while the Roman Catholic Church has been more at home with the writings attributed to the apostle John. Each of their theological orientations has its distinctive flavor and has contributed to the character of these two traditions.

Over against the Protestant position, Roman Catholicism places the source of authority in the magisterium, or the official teaching body of the church whose spokesman is the Pope. The office of the papacy can address itself specifically to matters of faith which are in dispute at any given time, thus providing an authoritative judgment which commands the serious consideration of everyone involved in the dispute. Protestants have no such authoritative office, but rather trust that the message of scripture is sufficiently clear to provide the basis for agreement in regard to fundamental issues of faith. Yet Protestants have divided among themselves many times over on issues which they have felt to be fundamental enough to justify division, and this disunity has been the scandal of Protestant Christianity. On the other hand, Protestants claim that their divisions are the natural consequence of a more priceless gift, that of freedom. They reject the hierarchical and legal character of Roman Catholicism in which theological judgments are imposed from above without due respect for the freedom of individual conscience. Most Protestants are not aware, however, that in spite of the legal structures of Roman Catholicism, there is considerable freedom of theological inquiry and diversity of theological opinion among its theologians, due particularly to the liberating impact of the Second Vatican Council.

The difference between Protestant and Roman Catholic views on what constitutes the ultimate authority for faith and theology is often characterized in terms of scripture versus tradition. Protestants affirm the Bible as the ultimate norm while Catholics affirm the tradition of the church as it is expressed by the Pope or church councils. Yet to oppose scripture and tradition in this way is to oversimplify. When Martin Luther emphasized *sola scriptura* (scripture alone) as the norm, it was a radical judgment of the waywardness of church tradition and the need to return to a Gospel which had been obscured over the centuries. The Roman Catholic response at the Council of Trent (1545-1563) was to affirm the integrity of the tradition, and this polemical situation created the false antithesis of *either* scripture *or* tradition, instead of recognizing their inextricable unity. Protestants during this century have increasingly recognized that we do not have the scriptures except within the context of our tradition, and Catholics recognize that the church's tradition has always sought to trace its continuity with scripture. We might characterize the relation of the scriptures and church tradition as dialectical in the sense that each provides an indispensable function in behalf of the other. The scriptures are the beginning of tradition and serve as norm and as source of renewal within the church, while the church is the guardian of scripture, interpreting it and enabling it to carry out its intended function. Each is dependent upon the other.

Both Roman Catholicism and Protestantism have sought to guarantee the validity of their theological authorities by attributing divine perfection to them. In doing this these churches have succumbed to the all-too-human quest for security. The Pope is understood as the vicar of Christ on earth, and his official proclamations of dogma were asserted to be infallible by the First Vatican Council (1870). Protestants, on the other hand, have attempted to understand the inspiration of the Bible so as to make it a divine document incapable of any kind of error. In both cases there is an attempt to erase the human (i.e., fallible) dimension of our response to the divine. There is a corresponding loss of confidence in the power of the Gospel to authenticate itself in the lives of people without having to rely on external sources which would guarantee its truth.

This brings us to the final point we would make in regard to authority. In the life of faith there is no purely external authority apart from one's own personal response to it. To speak of the Bible or the tradition as if they could be *imposed* upon the believer is to create a false picture. These sources *become* authoritative for faith as their message is received and validated in the life of the believer. For example, I do not believe that Jesus is the Christ, the chosen one of God, because someone tells me that the Bible is inerrant and therefore when it says Jesus is the Christ it must be so. Nor do I believe it because the Pope says it is so. Scripture and tradition must be united with what is commonly called the "testimony of the Spirit," or the personal response of the believer in the act of faith. This is a response that involves the whole self— not least our reason—in the encounter with the Gospel message. Thus scripture, tradition, and personal experience are all involved in the question of authority for Christian faith and theology.

Revelation, the Bible, and Other Religions

Our discussion of authority in the church assumes the reality of divine revelation. Revelation is a concept that is integral to Christian faith and to religion generally. It is a term which implies not only the reality of God but that God is hidden and is known through his being revealed. There are many ways in which revelation has been understood. It has often been associated with holy objects that excite fear and a sense of mystery, or a vision or illumination of a holy person, or some miraculous event that inspires wonder. In the Old Testament the utterances of the prophets were recognized as a word or message from God, either judging or encouraging his people. The prophets perceived in the history of the Israelites the working out of judgment as well as a promise of salvation which was never fully realized but pointed them to an end time and an ultimate consummation. These motifs of judgment and salvation express the biblical understanding of what revelation is all about. Revelation occurs in historical events as they impinge on our lives, turning us back on ourselves to face our limitations, our guilt, and our mortality. This is the self-revelation that occurs in the encounter of God with ourselves, in which we come to our painful moment of truth.

The very nature of this self-revelation turns us to the possibility of forgiveness and healing from a Source greater than ourselves, and this possibility is realized by Christians in their coming to know

Jesus Christ. The message and the destiny of Jesus conveys to Christians a sense of their own lostness, while at the same time conveying the presence of God as loving Father. Thus judgment and grace characterize the Christian apprehension of God as it is mediated in the person of Jesus. This means that revelation according to the understanding of Christian theology is a meaningful concept to the extent that it involves a person experientially in the realities of judgment and new life as they are made possible through Jesus. We can say that to find God is, at the same time, to find oneself.

This point introduces a dialectical or two-sided character to revelation. For something to be revealed, there must be one to whom it is revealed as well as the revealer. The Old Testament prophet revealed nothing to those who did not hear and respond to him, and Jesus also embodies no revelation to those who do not perceive in him a judging and forgiving Word of God. In other words, if I speak of Jesus in terms of revelation I give witness to something that has happened to myself; I am expressing my faith that in this Jesus I have encountered the ultimate (divine) purpose which illuminates my life. Revelation and faith are inseparably united, for to speak of one is to reflect the other.

We must relate these observations concerning revelation to the Bible, for it raises a question which is heatedly debated among some Christians today. In the controversy alluded to above between fundamentalists and modernists, we noted that a cardinal issue was the proper understanding of the Bible. Modernists went so far as to deny the meaningfulness of divine inspiration in the biblical writers and tended to regard the Bible as purely a work of the human spirit, not conveying a revelation "from above." Today, when the problem arises in most denominations it usually takes another focus. It is debated by theologians who on all sides recognize the inspiration of scripture and confess it to be the Word of God, but who disagree over what this means. On the one hand there are those who argue that the scriptures are inerrant because they are the words inspired by God and God cannot be the author of error. This is a view that was developed in the period of Protestant Orthodoxy in the late sixteenth century and which fundamentalism seeks to recapture in our own age. It would literally equate revelation with the words of scripture.

On the other side are those who maintain that the Christian understanding of revelation as historical events places the scriptures in the position of a *witness* to the revelation. The biblical authors are moved to write as ones who have encountered the risen Christ. Out of their own experience and perspective they testify to him as the one in whom God comes to us. Their writings are inspired by this revelation, but this does not mean their testimony loses its genuinely human character. They write out of their faith, and what they write becomes the vehicle of revelation because they interpret and communicate God's deed in Christ so that it addresses others as well as themselves. Everyone who testifies in this way—in every age—becomes a vehicle of revelation, but the Bible retains a special status and authority in virtue of its being the indispensable, primary witness. Its authority does not rest on theories of its inerrancy (which deny the genuinely human character of the book), but on the person to whom it points: Jesus Christ.

The scope of what we call the biblical revelation extends then from the revelatory event to the biblical witnesses, to their proclamation of the event as the Word of God, and finally to the believing response that Word receives today. In this understanding the Bible cannot be simply identified with revelation, but neither can it be separated from revelation. It is the essential middle point between the revelation event and the revealing of God within that event to people today. Within this context one can rightly understand the statement, "The Bible is the Word of God." It is clearly not *the* Word of God, which is Jesus Christ, but it is indispensable to the church in fulfilling its task of proclaiming that Word.

This consideration of revelation undoubtedly impresses many as terribly parochial. The discussion has been limited to Christianity, and what has been said betrays the Reformation heritage out of which I come. On the one hand it can be argued that this parochialism is not only appropriate but necessary, for we have maintained that whenever people speak of revelation they are thereby revealing their particular faith. But the question must be asked whether there is not more to revelation than the experience of Christians.

Is it not audacious to define revelation in terms of Jesus of Nazareth, a historical figure of whom millions have never heard? What about other religions of the world, such as Hinduism, Buddhism, and Islam?

Christian theologians have responded in different ways to these questions. Some maintain a very exclusivistic view of revelation, identifying it with the person of Jesus and stressing the uniqueness of Christianity as a revelation over against all other religions. They assert that in Jesus Christ God comes to us in his self-revelation, while the adherents of other religions are engaged in a quest for God apart from revelation. Theologians today, however, are not as prone to take this position. On the basis of our description of revelation, there is no reason to deny its presence in lives of people around the world. Shaped by the cultural milieu, the world's religions bring home in a variety of ways the dependence, the limitations and the mortality of the human race, calling upon their adherents to reflect on these realities in a spirit of humility and resignation. This experience can of course also take place apart from adherence to a religious tradition, though the religious traditions of one's culture will likely shape the way in which one experiences this self-illumination. This is the negative side of revelation which involves an illumination of human life in the helplessness of one's condition.

The message of grace, or the positive message of liberation is also conveyed in various ways in the religions of the world. It would be presumptuous for Christians to deny this, and yet their own understanding of grace will obviously be governed by their vision of Jesus Christ. Christians are convinced that nowhere is the message of divine love and grace revealed as it is in the crucified and risen Jesus, and they will quite naturally evaluate every religious expression of the human race in light of their knowledge of Jesus. But at the same time, the revelation of God in Jesus should not be used to limit the freedom of God in his relation to humanity. "The Spirit moves where it wills."

Many Christians feel threatened when it is suggested that people who are adherents of other religions can be confronted by God through their worship and belief. Yet the nature of Christian faith itself constrains Christians to be critical of every attempt to bind God to the forms of their own religion. Too often the church has been guilty of a graceless imperialism when it has claimed an exclusive truth in Jesus. The church needs both a sense of self-criticism and the ability to listen to the truth to which others give witness. It is hardly possible for anyone to be totally objective or scientific in his approach to religious beliefs, and the attempt to be so among some academics likely reflects the loss of their own religious commitment. But Christian faith has generated an extensive tradition of self-analysis and critical study which is eloquent testimony to the nature of that faith. It involves an openness to truth wherever it may be found and sensitivity to the all-too-human pretensions which lead us to believe that our faith yields not only truth but all the truth there is.

There is a tension here that must not be ignored or glossed over. Christians recognize in Jesus the definitive revelation of God: "I am the way, the truth, and the life; no one comes to the Father, but by me" (John 14:6). Nowhere in human history do they find a more powerful expression of divine love and grace; nowhere else do they encounter a Word which generates such hope in the face of guilt and death. There is a *finality* here in their perception of the truth about God and human life so that it becomes the basis for their perceiving the presence of God in whatever form it takes, throughout the vast experience of our race. The finality of Jesus Christ does not limit the judging and gracious presence of God, but it does provide the Christian with the key to understanding that presence wherever it is to be found.

This Christian understanding of revelation and other religions does not mean that doctrines are unimportant. It does not mean that all religions take different paths but ultimately lead to the same place. The distinctive content of the revelation of God in Jesus Christ is the grace, or undeserved goodness, of God. It is Gospel, the good news that makes all things new and generates a hope that transcends even death, the ultimate boundary of our lives. Wherever the healing power of this conviction makes its way into human experience, one can celebrate the presence of God. The message concerning Jesus Christ is the one known by Chris-

tians which clearly announces and communicates that healing power, and consequently they recognize the mission of the church in
proclaiming this Word. At the same time, they must recognize
that this God whom Jesus addressed as "Father" is the God addressed by other religions as well, and consequently they should be
open to them in a spirit of understanding and be willing to appreciate the riches to be found in the religious traditions of the world.
This can be done while at the same time recognizing the important
theological differences that exist.[5]

In these two beginning chapters we have discussed faith, theology
and revelation from a Christian perspective. If we were to juxta-
pose these three concepts, we would say that faith stands in the
middle, apprehending the revelatory event and expressing and clarifying its meaning in theology. The revelation of God in Jesus creates the possibility of faith because it brings a Word of judgment
and grace into the human situation that speaks profoundly to the
needs and aspirations of the human spirit, inspiring trust in the
One in whose name Jesus comes. Faith is moved to share this dis-
covery, to clarify and interpret it in such a way that it addresses
others where they are and confronts them with relevance and
power. Obviously these convictions involve an understanding of
who we are as human beings as well as an understanding of Jesus
Christ and the mystery posed by the word "God." We have touched
on all three of these subjects thus far; in the following chapters
we shall expand our discussion of each of them.

3

The Fundamental Question: Who Am I?

OW DOES ONE GO ABOUT ANSWERING the question, Who am I?
Perhaps there is no *one* answer to it, for obviously human
beings are so richly complex and so various that generali-
zations fail to capture the fullness of what it means to be human.
The very complexity of human nature inspires many different approaches in attempting to answer the question of who or what
we are. We can be observed through the eyes of a physiologist, a
psychologist, a sociologist, a historian, a philosopher or an anthro-
pologist, and each will give us a different answer to the question
because of the different angle from which each approaches the subject. When theologians address the question they also bring a
particular perspective, looking for things which, for example, the
physiologist does not take into consideration. But theologians cannot ignore the contribution of any of the other disciplines because
each has insights from which they can learn.

Many competing views of human nature result from absolutiz-
ing a particular perspective which is not comprehensive enough to
do full justice to our complexity. For example, a biologist may decide that not only are we animals, but any attempt to distinguish
ourselves significantly from the rest of the animal world is a mistake. We are then defined exclusively in terms of a biological
organism, and anything that a theologian or even a humanist may
have to say is regarded with suspicion. Or theologians may think
they have nothing to learn from what the scientist has to offer
about so exalted a creature as the human being, created in God's
image. It is this kind of tunnel vision found within both the scientific and religious communities that gives rise to the perennial

49

warfare between science and religion. Often competing views of
what it means to be human are at the center of opposing political
and economic ideologies, as in the conflicts between Western de-
mocracy and Fascism and Communism. Since it is helpful to consider a Christian understanding of human nature in relation to
alternative views, we shall briefly note several prevailing and competing anthropologies and bring them into conversation with Christian insights. In this way we hope to clarify and give an answer
to the question, "Who am I?"

Current Understandings of Human Nature

The impact of science in the nineteenth century went far beyond
the creation of new technologies and the consequent mechanization
and industrialization of society. It also involved new understandings
of human nature. This is not surprising for we recognize today
more than ever the extent to which the social and natural environment conditions the thinking and self-image of individuals.
In some way or another, all of the following views of what it
means to be human reflect the impact of new knowledge in the
natural and social sciences, which pose both challenge and opportunity to Christian thinking on this topic.

The Evolutionary View

Charles Darwin represents a revolution in the understanding of
human nature. In his *Origin of Species* (1859) he maintained that
life evolves from simpler to more complex forms through an evolutionary process which he described as a struggle for existence
and the survival of the fittest. In the course of this process the
human being finally emerged from a lower species. Christian theologians in the nineteenth century were threatened by this theory
because it appeared to deny our uniqueness as creatures of God.
On the other hand, there were those theologians who adopted an
evolutionary framework to understand God's relation to the world
and who argued that the lowly origin of human beings takes nothing away from their present reality as the crown of God's creation.
The theory of evolution does not pretend to account for how life

first got started (Darwin's theory begins with the fact that there is a variety of living things), so it constitutes no assault as such on belief in a Creator-God. But it did challenge the models which Christians were accustomed to using when they pictured creation, including the Bible's own story in the first chapter of the book of Genesis. The emergence of the theory of evolution is but one development among many which have compelled Christians to rethink and reunderstand certain portions of scripture.

Though biological evolution is a theory, theologians today generally recognize its validity because it serves so well in helping scientists to understand the created order. In fact, there are those who regard evolution as the indispensable theoretical structure for doing theology today. A prominent representative of this point of view is the French Jesuit and paleontologist, Teilhard de Chardin (1881-1955). Teilhard unites a cosmic evolutionary vision with Christian motifs, the result being a breathtaking synthesis which gives meaning and coherence to human nature and the whole creative process. The primary contribution made by the evolutionary view is that it brings out our organic relation to the world of nature. Theologians have often been unduly nervous about the intimate kinship between human beings and "clod and ape." Those tempted to deny this kinship usually betray an exaggerated spiritual view of human nature which distorts the Christian understanding of God's relation to the world as creator, as well as denying our essential unity with the creation. To grasp this unity helps us further to appreciate our dependence upon the environment and our ecological responsibility.

Having made this point, it is certainly just as important to recognize the distinctiveness and the discontinuity of the human species over against the rest of the animal world. When we define the human being we must focus on our *humanity* in order to get at that which defines us over against all other forms of life. Those who approach human nature from the natural sciences are often apt to miss this point. The writings of Desmond Morris (*The Naked Ape*) are a good example of the attempt to understand who we are in light of our animal ancestry rather than discerning what is uniquely human about us. His works serve as a corrective and reminder of our animal roots, but hardly provide an exhaustive answer to the question, "Who am I?"

The Behaviorist View

The behaviorist school is intent on applying the methods of the natural sciences to psychology. According to this view, psychology should not concern itself with the so-called "inner life" of the mind and emotions but should limit itself to observation of external behavior. Indispensable to the behaviorist is the observation of pigeons, mice and other animals in the experimental laboratory, providing evidence from which deductions are made concerning human behavior. The implications of behaviorism are presented in an engaging and provocative manner by B. F. Skinner in his book, *Beyond Freedom and Dignity*. Skinner maintains that our future is in jeopardy if we fail to exercise more control over human behavior in an increasingly complex and threatening world. Our ideas of freedom and dignity, however, prevent us from applying the kind of control that is needed because we think it is an imposition on the "inner self" that acts in freedom. Actually all of our actions are the result of stimuli from our environment, says Skinner, and there is no autonomous person who acts out of some inner will or purpose. Our notions of freedom and human dignity are based on an inadequate and increasingly outmoded understanding of our relation to the environment. We are products of our environment, and when we appear to act in freedom it is simply because the controls on our behavior are less visible. Our task now is to develop a technology of behavior which will consistently manipulate the environment so as to reinforce the actions we regard as good and discourage those actions we regard as bad. We are used to rewarding responsible behavior and punishing irresponsible behavior. With a more effectively controlled environment, the use of reward and punishment, which imply freedom of decision, will no longer be necessary.

One's first reaction to this proposal is that there is a considerable jump from manipulating pigeons in an experimental psychologist's laboratory to manipulating the world of human action! There is much ambiguity in Skinner's presentation as to how he is going to accomplish this, but apparently even this problem can be overcome by technology. What concerns us here are the implications of Skinner's understanding of human nature. We are understood as reactors rather than ones who respond and contribute to the shaping of our own universe. We are the objects of stimuli rather than subjects who act upon our environment according to goals and purposes which define us both for ourselves and for others. This is a crucial issue for the Christian (and for humanists generally) who sees in Skinner's viewpoint an assault on the human being as *agent* of one's action, and therefore an assault on the reality and the meaningfulness of one's own individual and personal self.

It is of course true that we do not act in a vacuum. We are conditioned selves who are always responding to and influenced by our environment. But to understand our selfhood as exhaustively determined by our environment is to turn us into objects that no longer possess the distinguishing character of the human being: self-determination. In his attempt as a behaviorist to apply scientific methods to the study of human psychology, Skinner necessarily proceeds from the observable world and then interprets human action on the basis of external stimuli. This is a much more "manageable" approach than to consider the elusive world of human intentionality and purpose. His method has its appropriate place and has contributed to our understanding of human nature, but its implications become frightening when the model of animal behavior becomes an exhaustive principle for understanding what it means to be human.

It is not difficult to recognize in Skinner a spokesman for a technological society that in myriad ways is assaulting the individuality and uniqueness of the human being. The Christian conviction that we are created in the image of God is an important bulwark in resisting these pressures. Our uniqueness as human beings is our freedom and responsibility, which places us in a unique relation to God among all the creatures of the world. Because freedom is a reality, we are creatures of destiny; there is a history and a purpose to our lives. Because we are free we are accountable; moral responsibility is the other side of freedom. Because we are free, the Gospel comes to us as an invitation, inviting us to a new commitment and a new self-understanding in our relation to God.

As Abraham Heschel observed, "Every generation has a definition of man it deserves." To a generation impressed with its science and technology, the human being will be seen as an object or the representative of a species that can be observed, dissected, and catalogued. But finally we must move from the question, "What is the human being?" to the distinctively personal question, "Who am I?," for it is the individual as subject rather than object that introduces us to a person's unique qualities. When one asks the question, "Who am I?" it is already an indication of the uniqueness of the individual human being, whose consciousness of self raises the question and wonder of personal destiny. Christian faith affirms the uniqueness and inherent preciousness of the individual person as a child of God, a uniqueness and preciousness which cannot be withdrawn because it is not within our prerogative to withdraw it. It is bestowed by God as creator. One implication of this truth is that the Christian should be sensitive to every dehumanizing force in society which cheapens and degrades the individual person, whether it be certain aspects of mass technology, or poverty, or political tyranny.

A singular character of the human being as subject is what theologians have called our "openness to the world," our "openness to the future," or our "non-finality." We are not simply "facts" that can be defined and circumscribed. We are not finished products. We are open to the future, beings in process who are defined by our goals and our aspirations rather than by our origin. This openness means that we are on the way to becoming who we are. We often talk about self-realization, which means that our humanity is an ideal for us at the same time that it is a reality, for life calls us to "become human" as human beings. Once again we must speak in a dialectical manner in order to grasp the two-fold character of our humanity. We can describe ourselves as human beings according to objective criteria—members of the species *homo sapiens* —and at the same time recognize that we are unfinished creatures whose singularity is apparent in our consciousness of ourselves.

This self-consciousness introduces the questions, the potentialities, and the values which orient the human being to the future and the quest for meaningful or truly human life.

The Marxist View

A nineteenth century view of human nature that has had profound impact in the twentieth century is the "economic man" of Karl Marx. Marx identified the economic organization of society as the critical social factor in determining human nature. Our work is the most important thing in our lives. In fact, our lives are defined by our work. Human worth in a capitalistic system is often reduced to an insignificant function, such as on an assembly line where workers are removed from the product of their labor. Since one's whole being according to Marx is wrapped up in that product, workers are alienated from themselves as well as from their work. The economic order of society must be changed if human beings are to arrive at self-fulfillment and overcome the estrangement they now experience. In his later writings Marx put greater stress on private property as a source of alienation, but this also is due to the capitalistic system.

In focusing on the experience of alienation, Marx shares an insight with both existentialist and Christian authors. But Marx is not so much concerned to reflect on alienation as a universal human experience as to concentrate on its economic and social causes and seek to overcome them. From a Christian viewpoint, his contention that an imperfect economic system is the cause of alienation is inadequate. Far more fundamental to the human situation is the anxiety which arises from our freedom and sense of mortality. Alienation and estrangement reflect the *questionableness* of human existence, which is inherent to our anxiety. In our openness to the world and the future we look for self-fulfillment, but there is no ultimate kind of fulfillment to be found in our state of existence. This does not mean we are consigned to self-defeat, but it does mean we must live by faith, which will move us either towards a false or an authentic destiny.

But Marx reminds us that our destiny cannot be understood in purely individualistic terms. We are social creatures, and to think of ourselves exclusively as individuals is to turn us into abstractions, removed from the social context in which we become who we are. A Christian anthropology can appreciate this point, without attributing such an exclusive and all-encompassing importance to the role of work. There is also much to appreciate in the humanistic concern of Marx, apparent in his stress upon the importance of human solidarity. We become ourselves in relation to other people, and if we live in a society marked by estrangement, the effects will be felt by each individual. The Christian understanding of the kingdom of God also expresses this unity of individual and society in its emphasis on our responsibility to our neighbor.

To speak of the kingdom of God is to introduce a tension between present and future, a tension which is present in Marxist thought as well as in Christianity. Both Marxism and Christian theology see the human being as *homo viator* (man on the way), for whom the future promises a fulfillment which will bring a final meaning and resolution to the human story. Marx's "heresy" was to secularize this fulfillment of human history, making it a goal to be realized through economic and social revolution and calling it the "classless society." Christians have resisted the notion that the kingdom of God is realizable through our own efforts, for it replaces the sovereignty of God with our own sovereignty. The consummation of the human story is not to be found within history, but at the same time it is identified with God's future as an ideal by which our own achievements are measured. The faith of Christians in God and their conviction that they live by grace means that their future is not ultimately dependent upon what they or their society will accomplish. Their salvation does not depend on what they can do, nor can it be identified with a particular social program. This means, among other things, that they dare never absolutize their own vision of the kingdom as God's answer for the human story. To do so is to become a fanatic and a destroyer in the name of an ideal, something that Christians have been guilty of in the past in spite of their teachings, and a feature of Communism in the twentieth century that has brought great tragedy to many who have stood in its way.

The Freudian View

The work of Sigmund Freud brought another revolution to our understanding of human nature. The conclusions he drew from his psychoanalytic method challenged the Enlightenment understanding that we are rational beings. This thesis actually goes back to the Greeks, where Aristotle characterized us as rational animals. In the Middle Ages Thomas Aquinas reiterated this view and it subsequently dominated Roman Catholic anthropology. As expressed in the Enlightenment period, the conviction that we are rational beings occasioned considerable optimism. Tossing off the yoke of religion and superstition, the enlightened person of reason was sure to create a world of peace and harmony. The notion of moral progress became a fundamental concept during the nineteenth century in understanding human history. World War I came as a great cultural shock to such thinking, and more critical and even pessimistic views of human nature began to emerge. But Freud's ideas have been particularly challenging and disturbing.

To Freud, we are more accurately creatures of instinct than creatures of reason. He identified the sex instinct together with the instinct of self-preservation as the two great driving instincts in human life. He later spoke in broad terms of a life instinct, which he called Eros, and a death instinct, Thanatos, perceiving the latter in expressions of masochism and sadism. Our celebrated reason is but the tip of the iceberg, what Freud called the ego. It seeks to co-ordinate the instinctual drives with the realities of life. Since we naturally seek to gratify our instincts and experience pleasure, our reason and culture in general is intent on restraining or channeling our instincts into acceptable behavior. Here is a picture of the human being as essentially irrational rather than rational. The Freudian view has been characterized as *homo lupus* (man is a wolf), an aggressive being driven by the need of self-gratification.

Christian theologians have carried on a profitable dialogue with proponents of psychoanalytic views of human nature. All of them maintain a depth dimension to human experience which reaches well beyond our conscious awareness, but they differ in their interpretations of that depth dimension. The disciples of Freud have departed from their master in significant ways, but all have re-

mained indebted to him. Some theologians would maintain that
the psychoanalytic view corroborates the Christian doctrine of sin,
in which a "shadow side" of our nature leads us to rebel against
our destiny. In any event, as we shall note further along in this
chapter, no view of human nature is sufficiently realistic that does
not recognize that we are in conflict with ourselves. Though many
features of Freud's view seem excessively pessimistic, the category
of the unconscious remains a fruitful concept in helping us understand the complex nature of human motivation and action. At the
same time, we should not use the notion of the unconscious in
blanket fashion to undermine all our good intentions and altruistic
acts, explaining them away as rationalizations or selfish acts in
disguise. This route leads to cynicism for it denies the possibility of
goodness in human nature. To Christians it is a denial of their
conviction that God is creator and the creation is good. The enigma
of our lives is that we are at the same time capable of much good as
well as much evil.

Freud's work has contributed substantially to the emergence in
our own times of what Philip Rieff has called "psychological man."
He notes that we are primarily concerned with mastering our own
personality, tending to our inner life rather than to the problems of
society at large. We have no dream of the future as did Marx. We
have given up the possibility of finding an answer to the perennial
questions of human existence. Our questions are practical in nature,
directed toward the goal of a well-adjusted psyche. The path toward
this goal is not involvement in the world but withdrawal into oneself, the practice of self-contemplation. It is a quest for healing and
yet with the consciousness that there is no final healing. The best
one can do is strive for some measure of balance within the conflicts of one's inner self, a practical and limited program. There is
no longer a faith which embraces the whole world and bestows a
meaning and direction for oneself, a faith by which one can both
live and die.[1] These ideas have made a strong impact on our society
today, but we have argued nevertheless that the momentous questions concerning our lives and destiny have not gone away. One can
ignore them or deny them, but they crop up in the continued uneasiness of life that is threatened by meaninglessness. The insight

of Augustine in his *Confessions* continues to speak to us today: "Thou hast created us, O God, and we are not at rest until we rest in thee."

Throughout much of our discussion there has recurred a theme which expresses the peculiar uniqueness of our nature as human beings: We are both animal and spirit, limited in space and time and yet soaring beyond our limitations through the use of creative imagination and intellect. We are both a part of nature and transcend it, we are of the earth and yet look beyond it for a sense of who we are. A characteristic common to most of the understandings of human nature we have discussed is that this transcendent dimension is denied, and it is no expression of exaggerated alarm to say that this denial threatens the very fabric and future of our society. If we are no more than evolving animals governed by an animal past; if survival of the fittest is understood in terms of animal warfare for survival; if we are viewed as billiard balls in reaction to our environment rather than people who act according to purpose and intentionality; if all the "higher" manifestations of human life as expressed in art, philosophy and religion simply disguise our self-serving economic interests as in Marx, or are reduced to the instinctual drives of the unconscious as in Freud;—if all of this is true, what is left of us? There are truths to be learned from all of these viewpoints, but if each provides the basis for a comprehensive understanding of human life, the end result is cynicism and despair. The sobering fact is that it is precisely these views, coming for the most part out of the nineteenth century, which now pervade and inform the thinking of the twentieth century. It is a legacy which seriously challenges a Christian view of what it means to be human.

From a Christian perspective, the transcendent dimension of human nature constitutes our uniqueness as creatures made in the image of God. It is our spirit-character, expressed in our capacity for self-transcendence, our openness to the future. Because we are this way, our lives have the character of a question that seeks an answer. The very question, "Who am I?" betrays this fact. The answer to that question is never totally clear and unambiguous. It may be that human life is no more than an accidental collocation of atoms, "a tale told by an idiot, full of sound and fury, signifying nothing." If this is so, then death is not only the ultimate enemy but the ultimate victor as well, destroying the claims to uniqueness and destiny which the human spirit would make for itself. Our self-consciousness as human beings refuses to let us accept death in all its finality precisely because we cannot accept ourselves as mere animals. Our expectation and hope for some final meaning to the story of our lives compels us to reach beyond death. The greatest pathos in the question "Who am I?" is felt precisely at this point, and it is here that Christian faith speaks most eloquently in affirming the resurrection of Jesus Christ as a sign of divine sovereignty over death. The resurrection is the keystone of Christian faith concerning human life, giving rise to the conviction that the final word to be said about us is not the finality of death, but the future of new life.

Human Life as a Problem to Itself

Anyone who thinks seriously about humanity cannot avoid coming to grips with the fact that we are constantly involved in a struggle between good and evil. Perhaps some people are able to live apart from this struggle in a purely amoral universe of their own, but if this is so, one would have to question their humanity. For people who think seriously about life, the conclusion is difficult to avoid that we are a problem to ourselves. The Roman poet, Ovid, states the problem frankly: "I see and approve the better things, but follow worse." The apostle Paul's candid self-assessment is much the same: "I do not understand my own actions. For I do not do what I want, but I do the very thing I hate" (Rom. 7:15). This character of human life can be analyzed and understood from a variety of perspectives by social scientists, but the theologian seeks to bring insight and clarity to human self-understanding by approaching the problem from the vantage point of faith. This brings us to an often misused and misunderstood word, *sin*.

The Concept of Sin

Sin is a concept that has both moral and religious significance. It denotes moral evil, but it also denotes a broken relationship between ourselves and God. In the former case, it is used in reference to particular immoral acts, called sins; in the latter case, it is used to characterize our human condition as we stand in the presence of God. Most people tend to use the word exclusively in the first sense, and the frequent result is that sin is trivialized by being associated with relatively petty misdeeds. In the Christian tradition, most attention has been given to sin in the second use of the word, not only because in this sense something quite profound and important concerning the human condition is being said, but also because the understanding of the human being as sinner is a correlate to the Christian understanding of Jesus Christ as Savior. In other words, Christians find the Gospel of Jesus Christ to be a powerful and meaningful message because it speaks to them as sinners, and meets them at the point where they recognize this.

The term most often used in Christian anthropology to express the meaning of sin is *pride*. The word is not used in the sense in which we speak of some people being proud and others not, but rather as a general observation concerning the self-centeredness of human nature that divides and destroys human relationships. In the words of theologian Reinhold Niebuhr, pride is "the general inclination of all men to overestimate their virtues, powers and achievements." Thus pride can be most offensively present in the "good" rather than the "evil" person. While a justifiable pride in ourselves is necessary to confident living, this is an egotism which exalts ourselves over others and even over God. Pride divides us absolutely from each other, expressing human pretensions which cannot suffer being challenged. Theologians have noted that pride can also be expressed in *apathy*, or the refusal to be anything but indifferent to the needs of others. Self-centeredness cuts us off both from our neighbor who would challenge us and from our neighbor who is in need of us.

Fundamental to these observations is the presence of *anxiety* in the human situation. Psychologists as well as theologians have been impressed with the quest for security that characterizes human life; we seem to be driven to achieve, to establish ourselves, to find security in a variety of ways. This phenomenon reflects the anxiety that is inherent to our mortal existence. We chafe against the limitations we experience in life, but our anxiety is ultimately rooted in that final limitation which is most threatening, the fact that we are mortal. In the face of death we are anxious and seek to secure ourselves, and this brings forth the pride which places us not only against our neighbor but against God. Here the full dimension of pride becomes apparent; in our desire for security we would make gods of ourselves, denying our limitations and dependence upon a power greater than ourselves. The sensitivity of the Greeks to this dimension of human life is seen in the drama, *Prometheus Unbound,* where Prometheus exhibits both the power and the fatal flaw of human nature in his attempt to usurp the place of the gods. Our sinfulness is not our finitude, but the attempt to overcome our finitude by challenging the sovereignty of God.

This understanding of pride leads theologians to express the theological meaning of pride in terms of *unbelief.* If sin is our effort to take complete control of our life and destiny, that means that sin is to be ultimately understood as unwillingness to place our life in the "hands of God" and to acknowledge his sovereignty. This is sin as unbelief, or a refusal to trust in God. Human nature does not readily come to terms with the sovereignty of God and our total dependence upon him. We portray the human being as a heroic figure, standing tall, looking with confidence into the future. But the Christian faith helps us recognize that our promise and potential as human beings begins when we fall on our knees. It is this profound reassessment of self in relation to God that teaches us that life is a gift, and that we live by grace. This is the conviction of faith.

In the preceding paragraphs we have been discussing sin as a condition of human life, or a situation that characterizes our relation to others. The term used in Christian theology to account for this predicament is *original sin* (over against *actual sin,* or sin as act). This concept, which has a long and controversial history, introduces the story of Adam and Eve as the account of the origin of our sinful condition. In order to understand what is being said in the notion of original sin, we must consider it together with the story of the *fall.*

Original Sin and the Fall

The principal figure in the development of the doctrine of original sin is Augustine (354-430), a native of North Africa and one of the most influential theologians in the history of the church. Augustine took issue with the monk, Pelagius, who maintained that upright pagans before the time of Christ were capable of having arrived at perfection. His view of sin was act-centered, and he regarded the human being as standing between good and evil in a neutral position rather than being inclined toward sin. Augustine feared that if sin is not inherent to our very being, then some would not need the Gospel of Jesus Christ. His reply to Pelagius was that sin is universal by necessity; in virtue of our birth we are sinners. How is this so? The answer, said Augustine, is to be found in the story of Adam and Eve (Genesis 3), the parents of our race. Their sin resulted in the corruption of human nature, and that corrupt nature has been transmitted to all of us through procreation. This understanding of original sin as hereditary sin has generally characterized Christian anthropology, finding typical expression in the following words from a Protestant orthodox scholar in the seventeenth century: "Everything follows the seeds of its own nature. No black crow ever produces a white dove, nor ferocious lion a gentle lamb; and no man polluted with inborn sin ever begets a holy child." [2]

In previous ages there was no problem in understanding Adam and Eve as historical figures and the fall as a historical event. The story's unlikely features—such as a talking serpent—merely whetted the religious imagination of the faithful. During the last couple of centuries, however, our understanding of the story of Adam and Eve has undergone a profound change. We recognize today in the story of the fall a particular literary genre, present in other sacred scriptures as well, which theologians generally call *myth*. This word has become a technical term in theology, meaning something quite different from its colloquial usage which means false or fictional— "that's just a myth." In theology a myth expresses a profound *truth* about the structures of human life and our relation to God by means of an imaginative story involving God in interaction with human beings. The myth of the fall communicates an insight concerning the human condition which is at the same time a statement of faith, illuminating temptation and sin as that dimension of human experience which brings God's judgment upon us by destroying both ourselves and others.

This means that the story of Adam and Eve is not an account of a historical event occurring sometime in the primordial past. They are representative figures, standing for you and me (their names are in fact generic terms standing for man and woman). Rather than placing them within history we place them at the beginning of history in order to shed some light on the nature of this story in which we are all involved. The writer is talking about the fallenness of life, the fact that life is not the way it was intended to be. He is describing the human situation by telling a mythic story, in which he is answering the question, "Why is life like this?" By addressing themes of temptation, pride, and disobedience, he illuminates the realities of estrangement and judgment and gives us insights which are as relevant for us today as for those of his own time.[3]

By placing the story of the fall in a remote history, the traditional understanding of the fall and original sin has placed the blame for sin on two people who stand in the past. This poses the problem of how to make the story meaningful for us, for their sin must be our sin and the distance between them and us must be bridged. The answer of Augustine was to designate the sexual act as the means of transmitting our sinful nature from Adam to us.

> Behold, I was brought forth in
>   iniquity,
>   and in sin did my mother conceive
>   me (Psalm 51:5).

The poetic and penitential utterance of the psalmist became a supporting text for the idea that sin is transmitted by procreation and is embedded "in the genes." This has had not only fateful implications for the church's understanding of sexuality, but unfortunate consequences for the understanding of sin itself. It turns sin into a natural quality which is received through heredity, just as I receive the color of my eyes or the shape of my nose from my parents. On the contrary, sin must be understood within the context of human freedom, which means that though sin is universal it is not so by necessity. It was not "caused" by something that happened in the past. Sin in Christian theology denotes the tragic mystery of life, interpreting the meaning of the fragmented and distorted character of life from the viewpoint of faith, but not providing a natural explanation of why life is like this.

As a concept which deepens the understanding of sin beyond the individual act, original sin also expresses the social character of sin. We are born into a society whose structures are penetrated by the disorder of pride and greed, and often the most extreme expressions of sinful humanity are found in its communal or social dimensions which can overpower the individual. This does not mean the individual is innocent, the victim of evil social structures (as in Marxism and much liberal thought). Individual and corporate evil are intertwined and mutually reinforcing, involving our individual will and purposes as well as the environment to which we respond. The solidarity of the human race is a solidarity in sin which impresses us with both the universality and the apparent inevitability of moral evil.

Several misconceptions concerning original sin should be noted. In Roman Catholic thought, original sin has been turned from a concept expressing the seriousness and universality of sin into a particular kind of sin, regarded as "mortal" or deadly to the soul and capable of being washed away in the Sacrament of Baptism. In the realism typical of Roman Catholic thought, this sin is understood as a stain on the soul which can only be erased by the sacrament. Original sin thus becomes a particular but peculiar sin in addition to actual sin, losing the conceptual force that we have been discussing. Protestant thought generally has not divided original sin from actual sin, but has regarded the former as expressing the full significance of the latter. The questionable tendency among Protestants has been to drive home the seriousness of sin with such vengeance that they have been accused of an excessively pessimistic view of human nature. A term such as "total depravity," for example, which is seen in both Lutheran and Reformed theology, has appalled Christians in other traditions as well as those outside of

Christianity. The point of the term is to maintain our utter inability to make ourselves right with God; we are totally dependent on grace. But the term itself is overdrawn and misleading. Some Protestant theologians went so far as to liken the human being to a stick or a stone in order to maintain the sovereignty of divine grace and one's inability to contribute anything to one's own salvation. These theologians mistakenly assumed that our freedom stands in competition with divine grace, when actually it is the prerequisite to any meaningful understanding of grace.

The Demonic in Human Experience

In addressing the realities of sin and temptation the question naturally arises, "What about the devil?" The Christian tradition has spoken of the devil, but does that idea have anything important and essential to say to us today? Despite a continuing fascination on the part of the public with diabolical themes in human life, most references to the devil as a metaphysical being tend to trivialize him. We do not take the devil seriously, but we are impressed with dimensions of life which can best be described as demonic, or "devilish." It is this sense of the power of evil in human experience which provides the meaningful context for any reference to the devil, but many Christians today see little if any value in bringing the devil into the discussion.

It is probably true that John Milton's *Paradise Lost* has done more to inform the public consciousness about the devil than the Bible itself. References to the origin of the devil in the Bible are meager and rather oblique, reflecting the religious mythology of the centuries preceding the time of Jesus. In Isaiah 14:12-15 we read about the "morning star" who was thrown into the pit for trying to usurp the place of God, and in the apocryphal book of Enoch there is material concerning fallen angels. Similar ideas are seen in 2 Peter, Jude, and the book of Revelation in the New Testament. The Bible does not teach a metaphysical dualism as in the Zoroastrian religion, where there are two gods of equal power, one good and the other evil. Consequently the origin of evil is understood as the corruption of what is good, or a fall from a state of goodness to a state of evil. Because we as human beings are created in the image of God, the source of evil is posited outside ourselves in a personal power which challenges the purposes of God. The devil thus expresses the reality of evil in the world and its challenge to every expression of the kingdom of God among us, and reflects as well the human experience of temptation in which we experience a divided self, succumbing to a power which is foreign to our "better self."

The church's teaching about the devil constitutes no article of belief, such as belief in God. There is no witness to a revelation of the devil in scripture nor even a developed teaching concerning the devil, and the Christian tradition has never recognized an ontological or cosmological necessity to the devil as we find in arguments for the existence of God. Belief in the devil was common in previous centuries—Jesus himself reflects his times in talking about Satan—but today the value of any talk about the devil depends on whether it helps us understand the powers of evil with which we struggle, both corporately and individually. Perhaps the better language to use is "demonic power" to express the nature of evil as a fascinating and mysterious power which can enslave and destroy us. Just as we can surrender ourselves to the holy, we can also surrender ourselves to the powers of evil in the world. The apostle Paul speaks of "principalities" and "powers" which would separate us from God, and we might characterize those powers as demonic, whether they be political, economic, military, or any other kind of power which would destroy us.

The Unity and Destiny of Human Existence

Every understanding of human life must bring together in some manner the two-fold character of body and mind or body and spirit which constitutes our human nature. We noted above that some views of that nature would emphasize the bodily or animal dimension to the virtual exclusion of our soul or spirit-character, while other views can be equally guilty in isolating and exalting the soul and either implicitly or explicitly denigrating the body. I suggested that the uniqueness of our humanity is to be found in our self-consciousness and freedom and not in the fact that we are physical organisms and as such related to the animal kingdom. But this leaves too much unsaid, and we must turn now more directly to the question of how to relate this two-fold dimension of human life.

The Distinction between Soul and Body

The concept of soul has played a most important role in Christian anthropology. It is a word which we more or less take for granted; yet it is difficult to nail down a specific meaning for it. It is an immensely complex word, receiving a variety of interpretations in the history of philosophy and even within the history of Christian thought. It has designated the vitality or life-force which characterizes not only human beings but animals and plants, over against the inanimate world. It has also been used to designate the source of human consciousness, what one might call the self. And it has been understood as a spiritual substance which provides the basis for our survival beyond death and the dissolution of the body. The last understanding probably expresses that of most Christians today, for whom the soul is a religious term embodying the hope of immortality.

Clearly the concept of soul has been used to cover a variety of human experiences, but most often it is used to express the peculiar character or uniqueness of human life. When soul is used in this way, it becomes an expression of the spirit-dimension of human existence. This spirit-dimension has been addressed in our discussion of freedom and responsibility, our capacity for self-transcendence, our openness to the future and our sense of purpose and destiny. From a Christian viewpoint, to speak of the human being as spirit or soul also expresses the capacity of communion with God and a life of faith. But rather than functioning as a concept which captures these dimensions which are unique to human beings, most people understand soul to designate an entity or object which is located inside of us. To understand the word this way is to *reify,* or to make an object out of a concept. This is an understandable development, for we treat the word "soul" as a noun and thus assume it must designate something. But this practice has occasioned considerable confusion as illustrated by the philosopher Descartes, who placed the soul in the pineal gland! The alternative is to understand soul (or spirit) as a functional term, a concept which expresses something of the richness of human beings, and which helps us interpret our experiences in the light of our convictions. This is what the word "soul" does.

In the philosophy of the ancient Greeks, notably in Plato, the soul was understood as an immortal substance which insured one's existence beyond death. This is certainly a principal function of the term within the Christian tradition as well. This view has resulted in a dualistic understanding of human life, reflected in Augustine's assertion that the human being is a "rational soul using a mortal and earthly body." This divides our being into two distinct parts, a soul and a body, with the soul being our essence and the body being a necessary accessory in order to get along in a physical world. This dualism of soul and body becomes the basis for understanding the existential conflict between good and evil as well, with the soul identified with good and the body with evil. In more recent times biblical scholars have challenged this dualistic anthropology, pointing out that on the basis of scripture the Judaeo-Christian emphasis on unity should take precedence over the dualism of Greek thought. The Old Testament in particular does not dichotomize human nature, but uses many words derived from the body (heart, breath, bowels, loins, etc.) to express the richness of human experience. Though one can see some Hellenistic influence in the New Testament, it nevertheless conveys a view of human existence which is basically derived from the Old Testament.

We have noted above that the spirit-dimension of human life constitutes its uniqueness, but we must now balance that assertion by saying that the body is integral to that dimension because human personality is inconceivable apart from it. We can speak of spirit or soul and provide definitions of them which will convey various nuances, but we are assuming throughout that we are speaking of human beings whose uniqueness is expressed in and through their bodily reality. The temptation of Christian anthropology is to stress our spiritual uniqueness in such a way that the spirit is isolated from the body, and we are understood apart from our bodies as well as apart from the physical and social environment in which we live. Christian theologians today are seeking to regain a proper understanding of our psychosomatic unity, as well as to see us in the context of our environment to which we respond and through which we come to an understanding of ourselves.

The Ultimate Question: Human Destiny

Anyone who considers the question of human identity cannot but be impressed with the wonder of the human being. Indeed, from a Christian point of view it is appropriate to speak of the mystery of human life, for we are in a position where no final and definitive answer can be given to the question, "Who am I?" This is so because the question ultimately drives us to consider our destiny beyond death. Is our destiny death—and extinction? Or is it the transformation of life into something new beyond death? How can we really say who we are until we know the answer to this question? Yet the possibility of a conclusive answer is not possible because the conditions for proof do not obtain for us until after we have died, when it is too late to report the results![4]

We are so constituted that we must raise the question of destiny beyond death. It is characteristic of human hope that it reaches beyond the grave, and consequently death has always posed a peculiar frustration and enigma to us. One could conclude with Albert Camus that this is but one more of the absurdities life forces on us, instilling a hope where there are no grounds for hope. But the Christian's view of the future is indelibly marked by the mystery of Jesus' resurrection. Christian faith unites one with Jesus Christ in the understanding that his destiny has become one's own destiny. The resurrection-event (which will be discussed in the following chapter) in effect makes death the penultimate word rather than the ultimate word concerning human destiny. It expresses the divine sovereignty over death which opens up new possibilities beyond the grave.

In stressing the unity of our existence in its bodily and spirit dimensions, we reject the notion that the essence of our being is an immortal soul that will not die. The unity of our being which is affirmed in the scriptures goes hand-in-hand with the resurrection as that symbol which expresses human destiny. The resurrection encompasses the whole person in a state of transformation, not just a spiritual part of the person. It is also a belief which recognizes the finality of death in a way which the teaching of an immortal soul does not. In that teaching, the soul transcends mortality; it is not overcome by death. Socrates is able to greet death with serenity, for he sees it as a liberation of the soul from the prison-house of the body. The death of Jesus, in contrast, impresses us with the "deadliness" of death. Death in the Christian understanding is more than mere mortality. To use the language of Paul, death has its sting because it is united with the reality of sin and confronts us with the threat of judgment and ultimate destruction (1 Cor. 15:55f.). The possibility of new life—transformed life—is not a possibility for us except as a promise rooted in the sovereign power of God.

With the affirmation of Christian faith that out of death will come life, the question arises, "What kind of life?" Too often in the past theologians have spoken with great certainty about the after-life, but there is very little that should or need be said. Reinhold Niebuhr accurately observed that there is little point in talking about either the furniture of heaven or the temperature of hell. It is enough to express faith in the God who at death will open the future that is beyond our powers of imagination to know or understand. The most important assertion of Christian theology concerning the life to come is that redemption and judgment will be brought to full realization, an assertion that is expressed in the symbols of heaven and hell. In speaking this way about human destiny, there is the recognition that we are moral creatures who are called to account for what we do (note how Jesus pictures the final judgment in Matt. 25:31ff.). There is the recognition that who we are is most significantly defined by our moral commitments, or the degree of our responsibility to the world around us.

But this in turn—as we noted in the first chapter—reflects the kind of ultimate commitments we make, or the faith by which we live. This gets at the real me, who is often difficult for me or any-one else to truly fathom. In view of the many ambiguities of life, the Christian is confident that human destiny involves our being known by God better than we know ourselves, which is a comforting thought. Faith awaits the judgment of a merciful God whose judgment can make all things new. The church has generally spoken too dogmatically about who is going to hell or who is going to heaven. The importance of these terms is their recognition that we are responsible for our lives, and that God is sovereign in his judgment of us. But our destiny remains a mystery which Christian faith awaits with expectation.

When one speaks of human destiny as reaching beyond death and the grave, many people (some Christians among them) become uneasy. They remember Karl Marx's judgment that Christian faith acts as an opiate for the people, whose attention is shifted to a life after death in order to be able to accept passively the pain and injustice of this world. But one must be careful about judging all talk of a future life as pie-in-the-sky. On the contrary, an understanding of human existence that sees its destiny as transcending this life gives an ultimate importance to what we are doing here. It places this life in the perspective of eternity, giving it a depth of meaning and purpose which is consistently being challenged. It measures this life in terms of the kingdom of God which captures the ultimate destiny and meaning of human life. It is true that in the history of the church, an after-life has often been interpreted in such a way that it has encouraged withdrawal from the world. It is just as true, however, that a Christian appreciation of the full dimension of our destiny has tended to sacralize this world and impel Christians to a higher degree of responsibility in view of their eternal destiny.

In considering human life and destiny from the perspective of Christian faith, we have inevitably spoken of Jesus Christ and the God whom he called "Father." In doing this we have said some things which need to be more fully explained. In the next two chapters we shall try to spell out the meaning of Jesus as we look more closely at who he is and what it is that the Christian sees happening in his life, death, and resurrection.

4

Jesus
and His Resurrection

F
ROM A CHRISTIAN POINT OF VIEW, one cannot talk about the
meaning of human life without talking about Jesus of Nazareth. He not only bears a message which Christians recognize as coming from God, but *embodies* that message in the character and destiny of his own life. As such he illuminates the meaning of human life and becomes the focal point for Christian theology in what it has to say about God. This has always been
offensive to people who do not share this faith, for it places an
unbelievable importance on one particular human being. It is one
thing to recognize in Jesus one of the greatest moral teachers the
world has ever seen, but to claim that his person is unique from
all others, that he constitutes a revelation, that he stands between
us and God as mediator—these assertions go beyond what a reasonable person may be willing to acknowledge. They are obviously
affirmations of faith which reflect the experience of the Christian
community. Our first concern in this chapter is to note the peculiar
historical problems that are involved in the Christian faith concerning Jesus. Then we shall consider the unique character of his
life and deeds, and conclude with a discussion of the resurrection
which stands at the basis of the Christian claim concerning Jesus.

Jesus and the Problem of History

We can distinguish two particular aspects of the historical problem posed by the Christian faith. The one has to do with the character of the sources we have concerning Jesus and the reliability
of the information they give us. This is a problem which did not
become acute until the nineteenth century. The second aspect of

the problem has always been recognized in varying degrees among Christian theologians from the very beginning of the church. This has to do with the finality or decisive importance which Christians find in Jesus, even though he is a part of history and is subject to the relativities of history like everyone else. This is the "offense" of the Christian message which was eloquently expressed by the Danish religious thinker of the nineteenth century, Søren Kierkegaard. We shall take up each of these problem areas in the order we have noted them.

What Do We Know about Jesus?

Every now and then there appears a new book on the life of Jesus which promises some new and startling information which will challenge the church's understanding of him. Back in the 1950s, when scholars were sifting and digesting the information in the Dead Sea Scrolls which an Arab boy had discovered in 1947, several books were written which caused considerable stir. They denied the uniqueness of Jesus, claiming that the story of his life and resurrection was a rehash of an earlier story about a figure whose life is recounted in the scrolls. One of these authors has more recently maintained that biblical scholars have conspired to repress the data of the scrolls so as not to rock the Christian establishment. Other writers in recent years have presented Jesus Christ as most everything from a political revolutionary to a magician to a homosexual.

The question naturally arises, "What do we know about Jesus?" The only significant source of information concerning his life is found in that part of the Bible called the New Testament, and most of that information is in the four Gospels of Matthew, Mark, Luke and John. These Gospels were not written by historians as we understand that term today, nor were the writers moved by an exclusively historical interest. They were followers of Jesus, concerned to provide the Christian community with the materials it needed to carry on a faithful witness. Thus we are told virtually nothing about the man himself; the focus rather is upon his sayings and parables, his deeds which excited such wonder, and a few events which were essential to understanding his mission. Some of this material had already been written down and the Gospel writers made use of it, but most of their materials were likely taken from an oral tradition which Christians were repeating in the context of worship and witness.

It is clear in comparing the Gospels that they have used the tradition with considerable freedom. For example, what is told as a parable or story in one Gospel is related as a historical event in another; or a parable told by Jesus in one Gospel becomes an allegory in another in which the writer spells out an interpretation which he believes was implicit in the original telling (cf. the story of the Great Supper in Luke 14:16ff., which is undoubtedly the older text, and Matt. 22:1ff.). This freedom was governed by the particular purpose and concerns of the writer, concerns which in turn were shaped by the needs of his readers as he perceived them. Each Gospel clearly involves creative interpretation by the author.

It would be wrong, however, to conclude that the picture of Jesus in each of the Gospels is simply a product of imaginative fancy. Each writer is dealing with a historical figure who was remembered by a community that had been deeply affected by what he had said and done. There is consequently a concern to place that same Jesus before them. Particularly in regard to the Synoptic Gospels (Matthew, Mark and Luke), there is a common Jesus who is recognizable in all of them. As one moves from the Synoptics to John, one is impressed by the increase in theological interpretation. There is a marked difference in the theological language and style of this Gospel, reflecting a particular interpretation which had developed in the Christian community from which it originated. This mixture of theological interpretation with a historical interest has posed problems for those trying to determine exactly what happened. Whatever one's conclusions on this matter, it is important that we do not make unrealistic demands for historical accuracy from ancient writers who were not trained as historians. One can affirm the general trustworthiness of the Gospels and at the same time recognize their interpretive character in the picture of Jesus that emerges.

During the nineteenth century, much European scholarship struggled with the question, "What do we know about Jesus?"

It was during that century that the historical critical method of studying the scriptures came into full bloom, and the results were quite unsettling to the Protestant churches whose scholars were carrying on this work.[1] To speak of this method as critical does not mean its purpose is to criticize the Bible, as many have supposed. It is an analytic and heuristic approach to the study of scripture, which means that scholars attempt to be as objective and scientific as possible. The goal is a better understanding of each book in the Bible by trying to identify the author, the purpose of the author in writing, the party to whom he is writing, the date of authorship, and so on. It involves extensive knowledge of the languages in which the Bible was written as well as its cultural milieu. The results of this analytic work differed from one critic to another, but often the conclusions were skeptical and perceived by the church to be a threat to the authenticity of its witness.

This threat was most apparent in what was written about Jesus himself. In Germany there was a vigorous "quest for the historical Jesus," in which it was assumed that scholars could discover a "real" Jesus behind the layers of doctrine and sentiment imposed upon him by the New Testament witness. A few critics concluded that the real Jesus never existed at all, while many others who rejected the traditional theology of the church arrived at a Jesus who was more suitable to their own theological convictions. Their picture of Jesus was pretty much their own construction, making them guilty of the same thing for which they had accused the Gospel writers! By the beginning of this century, many were coming to the conclusion that it is hopeless to find a real Jesus behind the Gospels. The Jesus of history is also the Christ of faith, and any attempt to divide the one from the other does violence to the evidence we have about him.

Following World War II a new shape was given to this problem through the work of the German theologian, Rudolf Bultmann. Recognizing the centrality of the resurrection to the good news concerning Jesus, he concluded that the historical Jesus is not really important to the church's message and we need not be concerned to find him. The Gospel actually begins with the resurrection, not the life of Jesus. The attempt to get at the Jesus of history is not

only impossible but unnecessary. This assertion by Bultmann led
to another quest for the historical Jesus, but this time a quest that
was much more modest in its claims because of the chastening
effect of nineteenth century scholarship. The conclusion of most
scholars—including Bultmann's most famous pupils—was that the
real Jesus of history is both relevant to the church's message and
accessible to us in the Gospels. Through centuries of critical exami-
nation the Gospels stand today as documents which bear the ring
of veracity, and biblical scholarship has contributed substantially to
that conclusion.

History and the Finality of Jesus

The fact that Christians attribute an ultimate importance to Jesus
in arriving at their understanding of God and the human story
raises a further question concerning Christian faith and history.
We may satisfy ourselves of the historical trustworthiness of the
biblical materials and still harbor some doubts about whether human destiny can be so decisively affected by particular historical
events. Is it not presumptuous to contend that the key to the human
quest for meaning is to be found in what happened some 2000
years ago in the little corner of the world we now call Palestine?
Is it not more reasonable to suppose that our access to God is more
immediate and universal—whether through our reason or intuition
or a religious "sense"—than having to *hear* a message about what
happened back when and where?

Since that period in intellectual history we call the "Enlightenment," during the eighteenth century, there have been serious
doubts raised about the Christian view of revelation in the name
of an enlightened reason. The German dramatist and philosopher,
Lessing (1729-1781), concluded that universal truths can hardly
originate from what happens in history. History is accidental and
cannot be the source of truth, which, if it is truth, must be universal
and rooted in reason which is the essence of our humanity. Is the
possibility of personal salvation, which is another way of expressing
the possibility of a personal realization of truth, dependent upon
something having happened in the past?

These reservations on the part of Lessing were prompted by the

Christian claim that Jesus constitutes a decisive, historical *revelation* for all people. Although this appears unreasonable to a Lessing or any child of the Enlightenment who would make a sharp distinction between history and truth, the Christian claim is that history and universal truth cannot be separated. It is in and through historical events that truth is revealed and apprehended. The Christian believes that certain historical events carry particular power in their ability to illuminate human existence and thus reveal its meaning and destiny. The life of Jesus—his teaching, his deeds, his transformation at death—has become for the Christian the key revelatory event from which the rest of human truth and experience is interpreted. This is not an arbitrary decision but reflects the experience of Christians whose own lives have been illumined by Jesus.

As we noted in discussing revelation, when Christians speak of Jesus as the revelation of God, they are not denying the occurrence of revelation in the lives of people who have never heard of Jesus. People encounter God in a variety of personal experiences in which they are called to account, brought to a moment of truth concerning themselves, and renewed by an experience of grace. These possibilities are found and celebrated in one form or another in the teachings of other religions, each according to the peculiar history in which it is rooted. But Christians understand every claim to revelation in light of what Jesus means to them and to the Christian community. Nowhere do they find another Jesus, whose life, death and resurrection has become transparent as the vehicle of divine grace. Thus Jesus is called *Emmanuel,* or "God with us," and Christians cannot speak of human destiny or divine truth without pointing, finally, to Jesus as God's chosen one. Jesus is consequently the one who not only defines the Christian's life in terms of its meaning and destiny, but who also reveals the mystery we call "God." The one is inseparable from the other.

It follows that Christians are not looking for another "Jesus," which would be a contradiction to the uniqueness they ascribe to Jesus of Nazareth. They find in him a singular manifestation of the mystery of God, expressed in the uniqueness of his destiny. As the crucified and resurrected one, his whole life stands as one powerful and ultimate Word of God, illuminating the human condition and its possibilities. It is this fact which accounts for the persuasiveness and staying power of the church's message. Another way one might express this is to say that the life of Jesus as a particular historical event (climaxing in death and resurrection) is a particularity of history which transcends history in the universal truth which it embodies or reveals. To more fully understand such a claim we must look more closely at the message and deeds of Jesus, as well as what happened to him.

The Message and Deeds of Jesus

Before we discuss the ministry of Jesus, some comment should be made in regard to methodological problems. The development of literary and historical scholarship in the study of ancient documents has enabled us to extend our knowledge dramatically concerning the cultural and religious milieu in which Jesus lived. We are in a better position today to understand the significance of what Jesus said and did as a result of these methods of study, and consequently the theologian can only be thankful for them and should be concerned that they be responsibly used in furthering our knowledge. At the same time, however, there remains considerable disagreement among biblical scholars on questions of interpretation for which there are no absolutely convincing answers. For example, one such question has to do with the cultural and religious background to which one appeals in understanding the New Testament. Is the primary influence from the Old Testament and Judaism, or the religious and philosophical ideas of the Greco-Roman world? Scholars are divided on this question which has many implications for one's understanding of the New Testament.

When I as a theologian make use of biblical scholarship, I am guided by the proven expertise of the scholar to whom I appeal as well as what I believe to be appropriate judgments on the part of that scholar in his interpretation of data. Here one's own theological stance will play a role in whether one is persuaded by a particular interpretation, and biblical scholars will often accuse theologians of being governed by their own theology rather than by the results of biblical scholarship. There is certainly a tension here that must be dealt with honestly by the theologian. On the other hand, the theologian recognizes that biblical interpretation is always to some extent in a state of flux and one's own conclusions need not be kept in suspension until the next book about Jesus is published. Whatever one says about Jesus' messianic understanding, his teaching, the deeds he performed, etc., one can expect that it will meet with opposing or alternative interpretations of many kinds. In view of my theological convictions I am attracted to those conclusions concerning Jesus which display both responsible scholarship and an interpretation of his life and ministry which is at least reconcilable with the historic understanding of the church's message. In the observations that follow concerning Jesus' message and works, we are concerned not to be exhaustive but to present a few basic interpretations and address some of the questions people often have about Jesus.

Jesus and the Messianic Expectation

We cannot understand the life of Jesus without seeing him within the context of the tradition from which he came. Jesus was a Jew who was nurtured in the Old Testament tradition of the law and the prophets. One particularly significant element in this tradition was the expectation of a Messiah (literally, "anointed one")[2] who was expected to be God's instrument in saving his people. One strain of the messianic tradition centered around the king. He was regarded as a mediator between God and the people, playing an important part in the cultic worship before the overthrow of the monarchy and the exile of the Jews in the sixth century B.C. The Messiah was imagined as an ideal king who would appear in God's good time as the fulfillment of his promise to his people, overthrowing foreign oppressors and restoring peace and justice throughout the land.

Another strand in the tradition was not as political in its understanding of the Messiah. It looked for a transcendent figure called the "Son of Man," borne on heavenly clouds and ushering in a universal salvation. It reflected the fervent hopes of an oppressed people as seen in Old Testament apocalyptic literature, which looked to the end times for vindication of God's purpose in history. In both conceptions, which undoubtedly influenced each other, faith in the coming Messiah was faith in the God of Israel, Jahweh, who was a God of promise and who would not fail his people. The Messiah was God's "man of the hour" who embodied the human quest for salvation at the same time as he represented the divine promise of salvation. Typical of Old Testament belief, this salvation was not understood exclusively in terms of the individual, but encompassed the total community with its social, religious, political and economic dimensions.

When Jesus appeared on the scene, he proclaimed the following message as summarized in Mark 1:15: "The time is fulfilled, and the kingdom of God is at hand; repent, and believe in the gospel." This message of the "kingdom of God," which is better translated as the "reign of God," should be understood in light of the messianic expectations of Jesus' contemporaries. Jesus is saying that the time they are looking forward to—the expression of God's sovereignty over history—is now imminent, and it is clear that his own ministry is related to its coming. Though biblical scholars will differ on the question of Jesus' messianic consciousness, I find the argument convincing that his message has to imply that he understood his own mission in light of a messianic conception. The authority he claims in his interpretation of the law ("You have heard that it was said . . . but I say to you"), his identification of himself with the coming of the kingdom, and his astounding claim that he possessed authority to forgive sins (Mark 2:5-11), all lead to the conclusion that his disciples were justified in regarding him as the Messiah. His idea of the Messiah, however, was not a simple repetition of the notions then current, but one that creatively transformed them. He distanced himself from a purely national conception of the Messiah, or one that was primarily political. His refusal to be addressed as the Messiah probably indicates this resistance to what he regarded as misconceptions of the messianic mission. It is likely that he did make use of the term "Son of Man," though here again his use of the term is enigmatic, sometimes indicating his own person and sometimes an eschatological figure who is to come.

There is a striking and paradoxical character to the self-image of Jesus as it is reflected in what he did and what he said. On the one hand there is the expression of authority and power, but at the same time his life is characterized by lowliness and suffering which culminates in his death and the events surrounding it. Perhaps Jesus reflected on the image of the "suffering servant" in Isaiah 52:13-53:12 as a fitting expression of his own life and destiny. In any event, the early church clearly saw the parallel. The kingdom of God which Jesus proclaimed is not inherited by the proud and the powerful, but by the meek and the lowly (cf. Matt. 5). It is no exaggeration to say that both in his person and his teaching, Jesus is revolutionary: Power is expressed in lowliness, sovereignty in service, victory in defeat. This transvaluation of values is identified with the reign of God which will make all things new. It was for Jesus' followers to see the final expression of Jesus' life and message in the paradoxical unity of death and resurrection which signalled the beginning of a new life (also expressed in the coming of the Spirit) for those who would follow Jesus.

A distinctive aspect of Jesus' teaching is the prominence of grace in his picture of God. By grace is meant the undeserved goodness of God which reaches out to restore and renew the broken life. The human response that Jesus' message calls forth is repentance and faith, or in other words, the recognition of judgment in one's own life and the decision to lay hold of a new possibility in one's relation to God and one's neighbor. This message of repentance and trust in God rather than in one's own righteousness led Jesus into considerable conflict with the religious "professionals" of his time, the scribes and Pharisees. Scholars disagree today over the accuracy of the New Testament picture of these religious people, and the legalism of their religion may be exaggerated in contrast to the spirit of Jesus' teaching. But according to the Gospels they understood their relation to God within a legal framework which stressed the observance of rules and ceremonial obligations. This stress on the letter of the law did not bring people to a recognition of their profound need of God's forgiveness and the new life which comes as a gift rather than an achievement.

A classic illustration of Jesus' message in confrontation with the Pharisaic mentality is seen in his story of the Pharisee and the tax collector (Luke 18), in which he reveals the insidiousness of religious pride and the sovereignty of God's grace. Both in his life and in his message, Jesus reveals the power of a love which reaches out to all people regardless of the judgments which we humans make. He associated with people who were publicly regarded as sinners, not in order to idealize them but to respond to the brokenness of the human condition wherever he found it. He scandalized the religious establishment by claiming the authority to forgive sins, an act which apparently he regarded as integral to his ministry. Both his life and teaching proclaim a "coming of the kingdom" which opens up the possibility of a new life for those who make the decision for it.

The Wonder Works of Jesus

Not only his message but also his deeds are important in understanding the life and mission of Jesus. When he began his ministry, attention was attracted to the mighty works he was performing, and it is clear that Jesus and the Gospel writers regarded these works as important in grasping his significance. This is because his deeds also testified to the reign of God of which Jesus spoke. Casting out demons and healing the sick were evidences of the authenticity of his message and the presence of the kingdom. This is brought out in a confrontation he had with the Pharisees, in which they accused him of casting out demons by the power of Satan, or the evil one. Jesus replied, ". . . if Satan casts out Satan, he is divided against himself; how then will his kingdom stand? . . . But if it is by the Spirit of God that I cast out demons, then the kingdom of God has come upon you" (Matt. 12:16-18). Given the kind of world we live in, the coming of the kingdom provokes conflict between good and evil. Jesus' deeds were an assault on the powers of evil that bind and defeat both body and spirit.

Jesus' deeds raise the problem of miracles for us who live in the age of science. Some Christians assume that anyone who raises questions about the miraculous character of Jesus' works simply reveals a lack of faith. Such an attitude hardly does justice to the problem, for it refuses to recognize how natural these questions are for anyone raised in our times. I believe it is helpful if we use the term, "wonder works" instead of miracles to designate the deeds of Jesus. It will help us to realize that the term "miracle" presupposes an understanding of the natural world which is unknown to ancient peoples. Since Isaac Newton we have understood the physical universe to operate according to the model of a machine; we can predict what will happen on the basis of laws of cause and effect. Though more recent scientific discoveries would challenge the simplicity of such a model, the fact remains that we are basically suspicious of any notion of human interaction with the natural world which would interrupt the laws of nature. This would be a miracle as we understand it.

Jesus' contemporaries held quite a different view of the world and their relation to it. There was much that was wondrous in nature and beyond human explanation. Furthermore, the line between human activity and events of nature was not so clearly drawn as it is today. This fact is obvious from various historical sources, but also from a comment of Jesus in which he notes that others were performing these mighty works as well as himself (Matt. 12:27). From this we can suppose that what the person living in ancient times regarded as wondrous and beyond explanation could be explained today on the basis of what we know. Perhaps some of the works of Jesus can best be understood on this basis. For example, we are aware of the psychosomatic character of many physical ailments, and some of Jesus' works of healing could be understood in terms of the psychological impact of his own personality and the authority which he obviously conveyed to his contemporaries. Yet these observations are not helpful in regard to those works which do not have a human subject but are directed to nature (multiplication of loaves and fishes, calming the sea, etc.).

During the nineteenth century many ingenious explanations were given for the deeds of Jesus. The assumption was that a natural explanation had to be found, even if it was an improbable one! Such an approach simply imposes in heavy fashion the standards of our scientific worldview without seeking to do justice to the biblical accounts. On the other hand, Christians need not feel they are minimizing Jesus' works or refusing to recognize his remarkable powers if biblical scholarship should provide some convincing explanations for certain of his deeds. For example, there are some wonder works that bear an obvious resemblance to certain wondrous deeds recorded in the Old Testament, and one could understandably conclude that these works are either creations or adaptations of the Gospel writer for the purpose of clarifying the person of Jesus as the fulfillment of the Old Testament story. The Christian should not be unwilling to consider this explanation where it appears particularly persuasive in regard to certain deeds. But ultimately we are driven to the question whether all the mighty works of Jesus are pure fiction, creations of the Gospel writers and have no connection with the actual life and work of Jesus. I would only conclude that this is not likely in view of the evidence. A powerful historical personality is not created by his followers; rather, they respond to him. One can assume that works of wonder were associated with Jesus from the beginning of his ministry. They defy any comprehensive explanation, and remain for the Christian as simply a part of both the mystery and the authority of his person. The really significant thing is how Jesus interpreted his deeds and how his followers understood them. They were signs of the coming kingdom that was manifest in his life and work.

The Cross and Resurrection

From the amount of space the Gospel writers devote to the final week of Jesus' life—the so-called Passion Week—it is obvious that they regarded the death and resurrection of Jesus as the focal point in understanding the meaning of his life. The other New Testament writers do not concern themselves with what Jesus did, but rather telescope everything in terms of death and resurrection. We can say that the climax of Jesus' life can be seen in terms of what happened to him: he was crucified and resurrected. Particularly in regard to his death, there seems to be an inner logic that runs from the character of his self-giving life to his death on the cross. The Christian community from the very beginning was driven to reflect on what it all meant.

A primary concern was to understand and interpret Jesus' death in light of the Old Testament. The Gospel writers were drawn to the "Servant of God" passages in Isaiah and interpreted Jesus' death as their fulfillment. The suffering of Jesus' life is redemptive, arriving at its ultimate expression and goal in his death on the cross. His death is also interpreted in view of the Old Testament cultus as a sacrifice which enables a new covenant between God and his people; particularly important is the understanding of his death as an expiatory sacrifice, or one that covers the sins of his people. Notions of ransom, deliverance and reconciliation are also seen in New Testament writings. Each of these motifs expresses the conviction that something profoundly important between God and the human family is happening in Jesus' death on a cross. The cross itself became a sign to the Christian community of God's love for the human race, and was proclaimed as such. As we shall see, Christian theology saw new dimensions to Jesus' death in the centuries to follow,[3] but it is safe to assume that the meaning of his death would not have remained a live issue at all if it were not for the resurrection.

Christianity has been called "the resurrection faith," for it was literally born out of the conviction that the crucified Jesus was raised up again. The Gospel accounts of the events following the crucifixion reveal a disheartened band of disciples whose hopes had been destroyed by Jesus' death. There was no expectation of a resurrection. When Jesus appeared to his disciples it resulted in a radical transformation from defeat to victory, from despair to hope. The resurrection thus stands at the beginning of the Christian church, for it made clear to Jesus' followers that God was indeed acting in his life and death. The resurrection was the seal of Jesus' mission as the Christ, the one chosen by God to bring new life (salvation) into the human story. That he was the Christ of God was inherent in his life and action, but the full scope of his meaning could now no longer be limited to the Jews; his significance was soon perceived by the church to encompass the whole human story. The exalted title of "Lord" (*kyrios*) was now given to him, for he was literally seen as the embodiment of God's presence in the world: ". . . God has made him both Lord and Christ, this Jesus whom you crucified" (Acts 2:36).

But the resurrection is far more than a vindication of Jesus and

the universalizing of the Christian Gospel. Inherent in this development is the reality of human death to which the resurrection speaks.
The drama of human life comes to its ultimate expression in the
conflict between life and death, and Jesus' resurrection became for
the church the final word that can be said concerning this struggle.
It has made the Christian Gospel a powerful affirmation of victory
over death and the meaninglessness with which death threatens our
existence. In other words, the resurrection of Jesus is not just a
"fluke," or another case of someone who appeared to be dead coming back to life. Rather, the experience of Jesus' followers was that
the resurrected Jesus expressed the sovereignty of God over death
and in doing so revealed the destiny of human life itself. The resurrected Jesus, writes the apostle Paul, is the "first fruits" of those
who have "fallen asleep."

New Testament Views of the Resurrection

Of all the events recorded in the Bible, the resurrection has certainly caused the most controversy. We all know that the dead do
not rise; can one believe that in Jesus' case we encounter the lone
exception to this fact? Is not Christianity on very shaky ground if
its message concerning Jesus is ultimately founded on such an unreal event? Within the Christian church today there are various
ways in which the resurrection is understood. Any responsible discussion of the subject would have to take seriously the New Testament materials and the understanding of the event which the disciples themselves had. Then a consideration of the assumptions that
were operating in the minds of the disciples about death and human
destiny is helpful in gaining a perspective on the resurrection.

When one reads the resurrection accounts in the Gospels [4] one
is impressed by the fact that no one witnessed it. What was seen
was an empty tomb and Jesus himself, who appeared to the disciples in a mysterious, transformed state (one account speaks of his
appearing suddenly through a closed door). The empty tomb and
the appearances are the evidence of Jesus having been raised, and
any investigation of the resurrection would have to focus on this
evidence. Scholars speak of two traditions which were passed down
in the early Christian community, that of the empty tomb and that

of the appearances, though of course in the Gospel accounts the two are united. In the earliest written account we have of the resurrection, from the pen of the apostle Paul (1 Cor. 15), there is no mention of an empty tomb but only of the appearances. This has led scholars to ask whether Paul was aware of the empty tomb. If he was and did not mention it, it would reflect his judgment that the appearances were most important in affirming Jesus' resurrection. If he was not aware of the empty tomb, it would tell us that probably the earliest accounts of the resurrection were stories about the appearances of Jesus, and the empty tomb stories were added later in dealing with specific objections. Those who maintain this view regard the appearances of Jesus as the primary datum concerning the resurrection, with the empty tomb spelling out the implications of the event and expressing the continuity between the crucified and risen Jesus. This does not mean that an empty tomb was never found, for one can suppose that if the body of Jesus had been found it would indeed have put an end to the claim of resurrection. But an empty tomb of itself was no decisive evidence of a resurrection; the body, after all, could have been stolen. It was the appearance of Jesus which gave birth to the cry: "He is risen!"

Though there are some discrepancies in the accounts of Jesus' appearances (for example, where was he first seen, in Jerusalem or Galilee?) and some obvious embroidering in the telling of them, it is difficult to argue away the fact that there was an encounter of the disciples with Jesus following his death. It is unlikely that they suffered an illusion or some kind of group hypnosis, or that they got together to concoct a story of Jesus' appearance. The impact of their encounter with Jesus was so profound in its generation of conviction that it is unconvincing to argue that the disciples were not genuinely addressed by the Jesus they had known. If one takes seriously the documents themselves, I believe one must conclude that Jesus who was crucified confronted his disciples in some form or another soon after his death.

Christians have long argued over what kind of body the resurrected Jesus had. Some maintain that for the resurrection to have been more than a subjective experience, he must have appeared in his physical body. Arguing on the basis of the empty tomb, they view the resurrection as the resuscitation of a corpse. Others follow Paul, who quite obviously saw the event as an act of God in which the physical body of Jesus was transformed into what he calls a "spiritual body" (1 Cor. 15:44). Paul understands Jesus' resurrection as no return to a former state, but as an eschatological act of God, i.e., an act which for a moment pulls the veil from the future and gives us a glimpse of what life will be beyond death. This transformed Jesus did not reenter the company of the disciples as if he had never died. He appeared as one who no longer belonged to this age. From Paul's viewpoint, one could well describe the experiences of the disciples as visions, just as he himself had had a vision of Jesus on the road to Damascus (Acts 9). This does not mean they were imaginary or purely subjective, but visions in which they were actually confronted by the risen Christ. In other words, these appearances of Jesus resulted in the resurrection faith; it was not the faith which produced the appearances.

Was It a Historical Event?

Another point at issue among Christian theologians is whether the resurrection should be regarded as a historical event. It was noted above that no one witnessed the resurrection itself; the evidence that pointed to a resurrection consisted of the appearances and the empty tomb. We do not really know what a resurrection is because it is a unique event unlike anything that we know. We can imagine a dead body suddenly awaking and getting up, but the Gospels do not give us any descriptions of this kind. If we picture the resurrection in this way, we must realize that such a picture is a metaphor or an analogy used to convey what we think the resurrection involved. What is actually described for us is what happened to the disciples: they were confronted by the living, transformed Jesus. This means that the resurrection as an *event* that happened to Jesus is something the disciples inferred from their being confronted by him. The resurrection as something that happened to Jesus in which he was "raised from the dead" remains a mystery to us, something beyond our reach. Thus the question, "Was the resurrection a historical event?" (or "Did the resurrection really happen?") proves to be a very complicated question. The important thing is that Jesus really appeared to the disciples; here is the beginning of the resurrection faith. The reality of his appearance is to the Christian the reality of his resurrection, or that something really did "happen" to him. What happened is obviously not a datum which is available either to the Christian or to the historian, but it would be wrong to deny the event-character of the resurrection on this account. It simply remains beyond proof or disproof. Christian faith affirms Jesus' resurrection as an eschatological act of God, recognizing it as both mystery and revelation to those whose lives are affected by it.

The inaccessibility of the resurrection as a historical event, together with the commonsense notion that dead people do not arise, would lead most people to dismiss it as an illusion. The disciples, however, were not only convinced of the reality of the Jesus they encountered, but they also believed in the resurrection as the end goal of the human story. The apocalyptic literature of their time pictured a final judgment and a resurrection brought about by the power of God. It was this conviction that enabled them to account for the appearances of Jesus in terms of a resurrection. Paul argues this point in 1 Corinthians 15:12f.: "Now if Christ is preached as raised from the dead, how can some of you say that there is no resurrecton of the dead? But if there is no resurrection of the dead, then Christ has not been raised." It is interesting to note how Paul subordinates Jesus' resurrection to a general resurrection. From the question he asks, it appears that some Christians to whom he was writing were more sure of Jesus' resurrection than of a general resurrection. But the idea was current and provided a way of understanding what had happened to Jesus. Given the nature of their experience, it was the most logical and compelling answer to the mystery of his presence among them: "God has raised him from the dead." For us who live in an age when human destiny is no longer thought of in terms of resurrection, Jesus' destiny confronts us all the more dramatically, challenging our times with the possibility that the final word is not death, but life! To affirm the resurrection of Jesus is to affirm the ultimate destiny of humanity in a future which transcends our powers of imagination and which is rooted in the sovereignty of God.

5

Spelling Out
the Meaning of Jesus

OUR DISCUSSION OF THE GOSPELS as the source of our information about Jesus brought out their character as portraits of Jesus rather than photographic representations. The writers were moved by the conviction that he is the Christ, God's good news to all people. In the New Testament we find a variety of ways in which the meaning of Jesus as the Christ is expressed. The attempt to spell out this meaning reveals the individuality of the New Testament writers, each using language and concepts that express his own understanding of Jesus and also express that understanding most effectively to the religious and cultural background of his readers. The writer of the letter to the Hebrews, for example, takes pains to interpret Jesus in light of the Old Testament cultic worship because he is writing to people whose understanding of God and the human situation has been shaped by that religion. A particularly intelligent and versatile interpreter of Jesus is Paul, the apostle (the one who is "sent") to the Gentiles. He was uniquely suited to carry the message concerning Jesus to the Gentile world because he had been raised as a Jew in a Gentile environment, and had absorbed the culture of Greece and Rome as well as that of Judaism.

The "Word" of God

The task of the New Testament writers, then, was to interpret the meaning of Jesus in light of his resurrection. The Jewish heritage out of which Jesus came provided the immediate background for understanding him, but as the early church became convinced

91

of the universality of his significance, various writers saw the need
of reaching out for other concepts and creatively utilizing them to
express what Jesus is all about. One striking example of this interpretive task is seen in John 1:1-14, called the prologue to the Gospel
of John:

> In the beginning was the Word, and the Word was with
> God, and the Word was God. He was in the beginning
> with God; all things were made through him, and without
> him was not anything made that was made. In him was
> life, and the life was the light of men. The light shines
> in the darkness, and the darkness has not overcome it. . . .
> The true light that enlightens every man was coming into
> the world. He was in the world, and the world was made
> through him, yet the world knew him not. He came to his
> own home, and his own people received him not. But to all
> who received him, who believed in his name, he gave
> power to become children of God; who were born, not of
> blood nor of the will of the flesh nor of the will of man,
> but of God.
> And the Word became flesh and dwelt among us, full of
> grace and truth . . .

There is a rich and varied background to this material. The
concept of Word *(logos)* goes back to Heraclitus (fifth century
B.C.), and at the time of the Christian era was used in Stoic philosophy to express the divine Reason which governs the universe. In
addition to this Greek background, there is also the Old Testament
tradition with its concept of Wisdom *(sophia)* by which God created the world (cf. Ps. 104:24; Jer. 10:12). These two concepts became interchangeable as Judaism became increasingly subject to
Stoic influence, with both Word and Wisdom being personified as
divine agents in creation (cf. Prov. 8:22-31). In the writings of
Philo of Alexandria, a contemporary of Jesus, the Word becomes
an intermediary between the transcendent God and the created
world. Philo's understanding of the created order as evil reflects
Gnostic [1] ideas, in which God is utterly transcendent and removed
from the material world. The author of the prologue to John's

Gospel has boldly utilized the Word as an interpretive tool in getting across the meaning of Jesus. It is obviously a risk because it can easily lead to misunderstanding. He does not intend all of the conceptual baggage associated with the word to be imported into his own use of it, but he is willing to take that risk. It is clear that his own faith in Jesus as the Christ has given a new content to the concept of Word, expressed dramatically in the closing verse: "And the Word became flesh and dwelt among us. . . ." The meaning of Jesus is expressed here in terms of an incarnation; in other words, Jesus was one of us, and yet at the same time his origin is rooted in the mystery of God. This "Logos Christology" was to have a profound influence in the subsequent development of the church's doctrine of Jesus Christ.

The apostle Paul used a variety of images in describing the person of Jesus. It is likely he had the divine Word or Wisdom in mind when he ascribes a preexistence to Jesus. It is possible that he also had in mind the Son of Man from Jewish apocalyptic literature, although he does not use that name. He suggests a different context in Romans 5, where he speaks of Jesus as the "second Adam" in stressing his saving role as the one who stands in contrast to the "fallen Adam." Many different titles from the Old Testament tradition are ascribed to Jesus by the New Testament writers, and in this way they express the exalted character of his person. One of the most majestic passages in the New Testament describing Jesus is found in Colossians 1:15-20, which tradition ascribed to Paul:

He is the image of the invisible God, the first-born of all creation; for in him all things were created, in heaven and on earth, visible and invisible, whether thrones or dominions or principalities or authorities—all things were created through him and for him. He is before all things, and in him all things hold together. He is the head of the body, the church; he is the beginning, the first-born from the dead, that in everything he might be pre-eminent. For in him all the fulness of God was pleased to dwell, and through him to reconcile to himself all things, whether on earth or in heaven, making peace by the blood of his cross.

It is important to recognize that every affirmation concerning
Jesus reflects a conviction about what has been done through him.
The meaning of Jesus' person, in other words, cannot be understood apart from his work. What he did (his ministry and works)
as well as what happened to him (his death by crucifixion and his
resurrection) were understood by Christians from the beginning as
both reflecting and vindicating his person as the one in whom God
is carrying out his purpose in the human story.[2] This conviction of
God's presence in the work of Jesus Christ drove Christians to use
language of divinity as well as humanity in describing his person.

One way in which two of the four Gospels express the divine as
well as the human character of Jesus is by telling the story of the
virgin birth. How are we to understand this story, and how important is it to the Gospel of Jesus Christ? From the discussion thus
far, it is clear that our consideration of the question of Jesus' identity leads us first to his life and ministry and his death and resurrection rather than to the virgin birth. The New Testament's own
treatment of the virgin birth restricts it to the nativity stories in the
Gospels of Matthew and Luke, though there may be some oblique
references to it elsewhere.[3] The notion of a virgin birth was com-
monplace in the mythology of the Greco-Roman world, and the
Old Testament itself relates the miraculous birth of Isaac by the
aged Sarah. Thus one can understand the "inner necessity" of surrounding Jesus' birth with the aura of wonder, and yet the New
Testament does not make it a central part of the Gospel message.
In the Gospel of John, where Jesus is identified with the divine
Word, the incarnation is expressed by celebrating the appearance in
history of the preexistent Word, without mention of a virgin birth.
In Matthew and Luke, where there is no mention of preexistence,
the incarnation is made possible by the activity of the Holy Spirit
in the process of conception. In both accounts the *discontinuity*
between Jesus and ourselves is clearly asserted. As a part of Christian tradition which expresses this discontinuity, the virgin birth
is a story that is rightly revered and celebrated by Christians. But
it is also misused when some maintain that without a virgin birth
Jesus could not have been the chosen one of God. The virgin birth
should not be understood as a biological prerequisite to the church's

teaching concerning Christ, but rather as one expression of the meaning of Jesus as both Son of God and son of man, expressing his discontinuity as well as his continuity with the rest of us.

Jesus as Human and Divine

As theologians in the church continued to reflect on the meaning of Jesus, the essential task was to affirm two things: the identity of Jesus with the rest of us, and at the same time the utter uniqueness of Jesus as that one in whom the loving purpose of God is being expressed and realized. In the ancient church there emerged two distinctive approaches to this task. The one, reflecting a kinship with Jewish thought, proceeded from the human Jesus and accounted for his otherness or unity with God in terms of his "adoption" by God at a particular point in his life. Most often that point was identified with his baptism, but some maintained it was at his resurrection. The other approach, reflecting the influence of Hellenistic philosophy as well as certain motifs in the Old Testament tradition, proceeded from the preexistent Son of God or Logos, and then accounted for his humanity in terms of an "emptying" of himself (cf. Phil. 2:5ff.), or assuming his humanity by being born into this world. The one approach moved "from below," while the other moved "from above." The former was most successful in anchoring Jesus' humanity, while the latter was most successful in anchoring what soon came to be called his "divine nature."

It was the lawyer-theologian, Tertullian (A.D. 150-220), who provided the church with its definitive language in describing the person of Jesus. He spoke of the human and divine in Jesus in terms of two natures, each separate and distinct from the other, the one bearing the attributes of divinity and the other the attributes of humanity. This duality of his being was unified for Tertullian in the concept of "person," so that Jesus is not two but one in his personal being. Yet Tertullian at times would describe the suffering and death of Jesus as involving his human and not his divine nature, while at other times he would speak of the "sufferings of God," or that "God was truly crucified, truly dead." It is not surprising that Tertullian stressed the absurdity of the incarnation, for he was uniting two natures which he defined in terms of their contradiction to each other, and yet stressing the unity of Jesus' person. For Tertullian, it was the very incredibility of it all which challenged the human mind to accept the mystery: ". . . it is credible, just because it is absurd . . . it is certain, because it is impossible."

It is understandable that theologians who reflected on the divine-human dialectic in the person of Jesus tended to stress either the divine or the human nature and then related the other nature to it as logically or persuasively as possible. The Logos Christology, which became the orthodox expression of the church's thinking about Jesus Christ, provides an interesting illustration of this. Its emphasis lies on the divinity of Christ whose "beginning" as the Logos or Word is in eternity. At Jesus' birth, the Word assumed a human *nature,* which did not mean that the Word became a human being like the rest of us. In the case of Jesus his humanity is not like ours, but is realized or completed in its union with the Word. However, to speak of the divine Word assuming a human nature without becoming a human being appears nonsensical to the contemporary mind, for the concept of nature to us is an abstraction that expresses the qualities of something—in this case, what it means to be human. For the ancient church, however, the influence of Platonism made it quite convincing for theologians to ascribe an independent reality to the concept of nature which could be assumed without actually becoming *a* human being. Needless to say, all of this appears terribly abstract when related to the flesh-and-blood Jesus whom we encounter in the Gospels!

The principal dogmatic statement of the ancient church concerning the person of Christ was adopted at the Council of Chalcedon in 451:

> In agreement, therefore, with the holy fathers, we all unanimously teach that we should confess that our Lord Jesus Christ is one and the same Son, the same perfect in humanity, truly God and truly man, the same of a rational soul and body, of the same nature with the Father according to [his] divinity, and of the same nature with us ac-

cording to [his] humanity, like us in all things except sin; begotten from the Father before the ages as regards his divinity, and in the last days, the same, because of us and because of our salvation begotten from the virgin Mary, the bearer of God, as regards his humanity; one and the same Christ, Son, Lord, only-begotten, in two natures, unmingled, immutable, indivisible, inseparable, the difference of the natures being by no means removed because of the union, but on the contrary, the peculiarity of each nature being preserved and entering into one person, not divided nor separated into two persons, but one and the same Son, only-begotten, divine Word, the Lord Jesus Christ, as the prophets of old and Jesus Christ himself have taught us about him and the creed of our fathers has handed down.

This statement comes at the close of centuries of often bitter controversy in the church, and it reflects the debates that had gone before. The four adjectives, "unmingled, immutable, indivisible, inseparable," are aimed at the dangers which were inherent in the two dominant tendencies of Christological reflection. These two approaches, which I have characterized as "from above" and "from below," were identified with two theological schools in the ancient church. The school in Alexandria, Egypt was the stronghold of the Logos Christology, while in Antioch in Asia Minor the human Jesus was the starting point. Some of the Alexandrians stressed the unity of the person of Jesus to the point that he was regarded as having one united, indissoluble nature which was divine—only in abstract thought could one make a distinction between the divine and the human. The Chalcedonian Formula rejects this view by saying that the natures are "unmingled" and "immutable." Among the Antiochians, on the other hand, some stressed the autonomy of Jesus as a human person to the point that there seemed no way to integrate the divine dimension, with the result that the two-nature teaching threatened to become a "two-person" teaching where the unity of the person was destroyed. The words, "indivisible" and "inseparable" were directed against this tendency.

Whatever the weaknesses of the Chalcedonian Formula, it did drive home the principal concern of the church concerning its teaching about Jesus Christ: one must speak of him in a genuinely dialectical or two-fold manner, whatever the difficulties. One cannot deny or blur this two-dimensional character of his person without destroying his meaning as God's revelation in the human story. The ancient church at Chalcedon did not resolve the Christological disputes by providing a creative, new synthesis. It simply restated the conviction that Jesus is truly God and truly man over against tendencies to deny one or the other. Ever since Chalcedon, theologians with a sense of responsibility to the historic message of the church have done their Christological thinking in such a way as to reflect the concerns of that statement. This does not mean, however, that one must repeat the language and concepts found there in order to be faithful to their intention. This is the point being made by contemporary theologians who are seeking to be faithful to the church's teaching concerning Christ as they present him to a world which is far removed from the philosophical language and worldview of the fifth century.

Contemporary Thinking about Jesus

There are many images in current theology which attempt to convey the meaning of Jesus Christ. This variety indicates the pluralism in theology today as well as the fact that our apprehension of Jesus is shaped by the perspective we bring to him. For example, beginning with the 1960s when many were saying that the church must become an agent for social change and even a revolutionary force in society, Jesus himself has been increasingly pictured as a revolutionary. His conflict with the political authority (King Herod) and the religious establishment is emphasized, and his kinship with the poor and critique of the rich is interpreted as social radicalism. Black theologians have emphasized Christ as the Liberator, whose own experience of suffering and oppression identifies him with the struggle against oppression in which minority peoples in our own country are engaged. Contrast this view of Christ with that seen in much of American piety, the "gentle Jesus, meek and mild" whose head is crowned by a halo and whose body is covered by a gleaming white robe. Or contrast it again with the view of the "Jesus freak," whose interests are more immediately centered on his own quest for self-fulfillment. One rather arresting interpretation of Jesus today is conveyed in the image of the clown or harlequin. The clown calls into question the way we perceive the world, suggesting a gap between reality and our perception of it. In revealing both the comic and tragic dimensions of life, the clown becomes the occasion for self-illumination and self-criticism.

But beyond the image used to interpret Jesus, there remains the central issue we have noted, that of understanding the uniqueness of Jesus as one who comes "from God." This is the central affirmation of Christian faith; how shall it be presented in our own times? Generally one can say that current Christological thinking is critical of Logos Christology, the dominant model from ancient times. In beginning with the preexistent Word who assumed human flesh, this view has made it difficult for Christians to appreciate the fact that Jesus was truly one of us. The heresy of docetism in which Jesus is seen as a divine figure who appeared in the human story but was not really and truly a human being, has been very close to most Christians.

What do Christians mean today when they confess (in the words of the Nicene Creed) that Jesus Christ "came down from heaven . . . and was made man"? When we no longer understand the universe to consist of heaven "up above," the earth in the middle, and an "underworld" beneath us, it is at least difficult and more likely impossible for Christians to take this language literally. For example, to speak of preexistence would imply a state of existence in a spirit-realm in which the Word "lives" prior to entering human history. In an age when the dominant understanding of reality involved spheres of celestial being transcending this world in which we live, the notion of preexistence could be literally understood without any problem. But today, if the word is to be used at all it has to be understood in view of its function, or symbolically, rather than as a descriptive term. Thus the Dutch Jesuit, Piet Schoonenberg, regards preexistence as a "temporal image" for transcendence; its function is simply to express the full meaning of

Jesus as one who is divine at the same time as he is fully human. To use the word today can no longer imply the cosmology which it presupposed in an earlier age, nor can it be used as an explanation for ascribing divinity to the person of Jesus.

But what does it mean to speak of Jesus as "divine"? Does not this word also call for some interpretation? Theologians today are concerned to interpret the divinity of Jesus in a manner which avoids turning him into a bizarre, mythological creature who contains both a divine nature and a human nature. In centuries past this kind of language led to lengthy discussions about such questions as these: Was Jesus according to his divine nature omniscient (all-knowing)? Could he have suffered according to his divine nature, or was suffering limited to his human nature? Did he really die on the cross, or was it just his human nature that died? These questions arose from the fact that the person of Jesus was understood as literally constituted by two abstractions which are defined as contradictory to each other. As both divine and human, Jesus was seen to embrace both eternity and temporality, infinity and finitude, immutability and mutability, impassibility and passibility. To place these antithetical attributes in one person (even if, as some have argued, the divine attributes are "emptied" without denying his divinity) puts a severe strain on the unity of that personality. It makes an unreal theological construction out of one who is clearly pictured in the Gospels as a genuine, historical person who lived a fully human life among his contemporaries.

There is a trend in current Christological thinking to reverse the direction of the traditional Logos Christology. It begins with the man Jesus instead of the eternal Word, and understands his divinity within the context of his genuinely human life. To speak in terms of a synthesis of the divine and human in Jesus, whether in terms of two natures or any other language, not only turns him into an unreal abstraction but also compromises his humanity because it is either swallowed up in his divinity or stands in competition with it. Is it not more effective, then, to speak of the divine in terms of humanity that arrives at its realization, or *fulfilled* humanity? Not only is this language more satisfying, but it expresses as well the conviction that a realized humanity is the goal of God's uniting himself with us. We do not dissolve the notion of divinity into humanity by speaking this way, but rather express it in the category of Jesus' uniqueness. He is one of us, and yet we recognize his otherness in embodying the divine purpose and demonstrating what it means to be fully human.

This fullness of humanity in Jesus can be understood in terms of his relationship to God, whom he addresses as Father. His relationship to God was one of total trust and dependence, a relationship which describes our own proper destiny. We noted in our discussion of human nature that our distinguishing character is openness to the world and to the future. In Jesus this openness arrives at its fulfillment. We can call him the "eschatological man" who shows us our proper destiny at the same time as he reveals to us the God of our world and our future. It is important to avoid the notion (judged heretical by the ancient church) that Jesus warranted or deserved adoption by God because of his own achievement, whether understood in terms of moral perfection or establishing his own peculiar relationship to God. Such a view would make the incarnation a human achievement rather than God's act. The mystery lies in the paradoxical unity of divine action and human freedom as they are joined in Jesus' life, by virtue of which Jesus stands in that unique relation to God which we have described in terms of total trust.

With this understanding of Jesus there are certain implications that follow in regard to his self-consciousness. We asserted earlier that he did have a messianic understanding of his mission, but we can assume that he arrived at this understanding in the course of his development as a person. To take his humanity seriously is to recognize a development in messianic consciousness, born out of struggle and gradually unfolding as Jesus reflected on the events in his life which were moving him inexorably to the cross. Also in regard to his knowledge of the world, we can no longer assume with theologians of the middle ages that Jesus had a supernatural grasp of all knowledge, whether past, present, or future. This claim was based on the notion that Jesus possessed complete perfection because of his divine nature. To take his humanity seriously, however, is to abandon this kind of speculative reasoning. It is to recognize not only the process of growth and development but also that Jesus was conditioned by the cultural milieu in which he lived. He was a child of his own times, even as his ministry and destiny were to so utterly transcend his times in the meaning they bore for the whole course of human history.

What implications does our understanding of Jesus' uniqueness carry for the church's teaching concerning his sinlessness? Since the middle ages it has been maintained that not only was Jesus without sin; it was impossible that he *could* have sinned. In the nineteenth century Protestant theologians raised the question whether Jesus' temptation (Matt. 4) was not meaningless and a sham if it was impossible for him to sin. It is of course understandable that Christians have ascribed sinlessness to Christ in view of their understanding of his work as Savior and his unity with God the Father. However, it is hardly possible to verify whether Jesus ever had an impure or selfish thought, and this is not the context in which the matter should be discussed. Jesus' sinlessness is a theological judgment rather than an empirical one in the sense of collecting all the evidence that would be relevant to a judgment, for that is not possible for us. To affirm the sinlessness of Jesus is another way to acknowledge his uniqueness as one whose life was lived in total dependence and trust. It is the negative expression of the affirmation made above, that in him we see the fulfillment of humanity, the realization of God's intention for us. This conviction could imply that he was a totally integrated human being whose life was free of those exploitative and self-destructive gestures of an insecure ego which characterize the rest of us. But the point in speaking of Jesus' sinlessness is to affirm the totality of his dedication to God the Father and the perfect completion of his mission as God's chosen one.[4]

What Difference Does Jesus Make?

With this question we come to the crux of the matter in our thinking about Jesus. All of the assertions we have made about him reflect a conviction that his life really matters in our attempt to understand what human life is all about. His uniqueness is not simply a phenomenon inviting the speculations of the curious and the superstitious; rather, it sheds light on the human story and opens new possibilities for us who are engaged in living out that story. For the Christian, Jesus' life constitutes a revelation from God which both reveals the human condition for what it is and at the same time reveals the divine answer to that condition. As one looks at the history of Christian reflection concerning the work of Christ, there are several views that have been particularly important in shaping the church's thinking. They usually center upon the cross as the culmination point in understanding the meaning of Jesus' life, and that cross is seen as an act of atonement which unites us with God.

Views of the Atonement

One view of the cross expressed in the New Testament is an obvious reflection of the Old Testament cultic system. It understands the cross as the ultimate sacrifice offered to God in behalf of humanity. Jewish worship included several kinds of sacrifices and offerings which expressed self-dedication to God as well as the need of being found acceptable in the presence of God. Jesus' death on the cross is regarded by several New Testament authors as an expiatory sacrifice, or one which covers our sins. The writer of the Letter to the Hebrews contrasts the inadequacy of animal sacrifices, which must be offered repeatedly year in and year out, with the "once-for-all" character of Jesus' death. Today, of course, the notion of sacrifice is far removed from the offering up of animals, and consequently to speak of Jesus' death in relation to this ancient practice is not very helpful in reaching the twentieth century person. At the same time, there is certainly an important meaning to Jesus' life that is expressed in the notion of sacrificial action. Already in the New Testament we see some creative interpretation of Jesus' sacrifice in terms of his obedience to his Father. The language of sacrifice is particularly strong among Roman Catholics, who have understood the sacrament of the eucharist primarily in terms of a "bloodless" sacrifice offered to God. But theological reflection on the death of Christ has utilized other motifs, some of which are clearly related to sacrifice but which are taken from sources other than the biblical material itself.

One of these views, which has exerted considerable influence within the Roman Catholic Church, dates back to the great Scholastic theologian, Anselm (1033-1109). In his book, *Cur deus homo?* (Why did God become man?) he maintains that sin has been a violation of God's honor and that something must be done to restore that honor. The concept he uses to denote the work of Christ in restoring God's honor is "satisfaction," a word taken from the sacrament of penance. That sacrament includes both absolution (declaration of forgiveness) and imposition of works of satisfaction. Anselm applies this practice to the cross of Christ, asking if it would be fitting for God simply to forgive our sins without some kind of restitution being made. His answer is that it would not. Consequently Jesus' death on the cross is seen as the means by which satisfaction or atonement is made and God's honor restored.

A dominant view of the atonement in Protestant theology also reflects the idea of sacrifice as satisfaction, but the emphasis is on the cross as satisfaction of the demands of God's justice. A quote from the reformer, John Calvin, expresses this view quite well: "In this situation, Christ took upon himself and suffered the punishment which by the righteous judgment of God impended over all sinners, and by this expiation the Father has been satisfied and his wrath appeased" (*Institutes of the Christian Religion,* Book II, Chapter 16). Because Jesus is seen here as bearing the punishment which we deserve, and because this punishment expresses the wrathful judgment of God, this view has been called the "penal" or "juridical" theory of the atonement. There are several more variations of the Anselmian and orthodox Protestant understandings of the atonement, all of which understand the cross of Christ as in some way answering the demands of God upon sinful humanity. They capture the vicarious nature of Jesus and his cross which is conveyed in the scriptures—his life and death are "for us." But we are left with a picture of God which is hardly true to the New Testament. He is seen as an offended or wrathful God rather than the God who "so loved the world that he gave his only begotten Son" (John 3:16).

As one might surmise, there has been resistance to these views of the atonement, dating back to Abelard (1079-1142). Rather than understanding Jesus' death as directed to God in an act of appeasement, he saw the cross and its consequences directed toward us. The cross demonstrates the love of God which calls forth an answering love from those whose lives it touches. This means that the cross reveals what has always been true: God loves us. Consequently, there is no need of propitiating God or reconciling him to us. There is need only that we return to God, and the cross assures us that we can. This view is often called the "subjective" or "moral influence" theory of the atonement, since the change brought about by the cross is in the hearts of believers who respond to it. Variations of this view appeared in Protestant theology during the nineteenth century. Many theologians of a more liberal stance found it difficult to stress the holiness or wrath of God and could not envision a view of the atonement which was shaped by those qualities. God is either a God of love or a God of justice; he is related to us either as a God of mercy or a God of law. With these exclusive alternatives, Protestant liberal theology opted for a God of love and mercy and ignored or rejected the themes of divine holiness which implied a God of judgment and wrath.

Another view of the atonement revived in this century by a Swedish theologian, Gustaf Aulen, sees the cross and resurrection in the context of the struggle between the forces of good and evil. The cross and resurrection, as a two-sided event, expresses the victory of God over the powers of darkness. The human race is involved in a dramatic conflict of cosmic dimensions. It reaches its climax in the cross and resurrection, understood as God's victory on our behalf over the powers of sin and death. The motif of victory is strong in this view, expressing the message of Easter far more directly and powerfully than the other views. Aulen sees this theme of cosmic victory ("Christus Victor") as the dominant interpretation of the ancient church and argues that we should recapture it for today. One can certainly appreciate aspects of Aulen's view of the atonement as well as recognizing the strengths and weaknesses of the other views we have discussed, but any one view of the atonement is inadequate in capturing the richness of its meaning. In the following pages we shall elaborate on some aspects of the cross which we think are particularly important to its proper understanding.

"God Was in Christ . . ."

The question with which we introduced this discussion was, "What difference does Jesus make?" This must be the starting point in our approach to the atonement, which means that we must move from the realities of our own experience to the cross and resurrection of Jesus Christ and then back again to ourselves, in order that these events may express and clarify the meaning of human existence for us. The starting point is the experience of brokenness, of guilt and the yearning for wholeness which characterizes human experience. In Chapter 3 we discussed this human problem in terms of sin, which expresses the Christian conviction that the warped and broken character of life is at root a theological problem. By this I mean that the self-centeredness of human beings which is destructive of both the self and the possibilities of meaningful community, reflects a rupture in the very purpose and goal of human life. Christian faith perceives that goal as having been realized in the life of Jesus, whose complete trust in God reveals the end purpose of human life. He is the flesh and blood realization of the fact that we are destined for God, and that destiny is recognized and anticipated in the faith which Jesus both exemplifies and inspires. But we are constantly reminded of our own estrangement from God, which we experience in the loss of our integrity, our lack of trust, and our apprehension of the future.[5] We yearn to be whole, at one with ourselves and with God who is the Source of our being. This quest permeates human existence and in its light we understand the death and resurrection of Jesus Christ. The cross and empty tomb express for Christians the reality of atonement or reconciliation between God and themselves.

Many Christians, myself included, are impressed by the failure of the church to give an effective witness concerning the cross of Christ. Its meaning is easily lost in clichés which seem remote from the realities of human life. The word "salvation," which is often used among Christians to express the meaning of Christ, has become so stereotyped that it is no longer a useful term. The question often posed in evangelistic fervor, "Are you saved, brother?" leaves us with the impression that to be saved is to embark on a parochial and unexciting life. This situation is tragic in view of the fact that the message of the cross actually touches the most profound levels of human existence. To be saved is to find ourselves, but only because we find a liberating Word of forgiveness and hope which comes from a Source greater than ourselves.

Once again we should note the importance of historical events to Christian faith. To say that "God is love" is not simply to speak of an idea, but to recognize the expression of divine love in the cross of Christ. In his uniqueness as one in whom God's presence is expressed and realized, he becomes for us a representative figure whose life embodies our life before God. In him, faith perceives that *God is for us.* What happened to Jesus tells us that the alienating and destructive power of evil in our lives and in the world around us is not the final word. In his suffering we see the power of redemptive love which is able to transform death into life, defeat into victory. This is the essential message of the early church, and it is expressed in the witness of the apostles that the cross demonstrates God's love for sinful human beings: "God shows his love for us in that while we were yet sinners, Christ died for us" (Rom. 5:8). His death encompasses our death because of his own unique destiny: in him the realities of judgment and grace meet and define our own destiny as well as his. That destiny is that we be reconciled to God: "God was in Christ, reconciling the world to himself" (2 Cor. 5:19).

The problem of many views of the atonement is that they picture it as a cosmic transaction without relating it to the personal experience of reconciliation. Moreover they tend to mistakenly stress either the justice and holiness of God or the love of God, without properly relating these motifs to each other. The first approach makes it appear that God must first be appeased or satisfied before he is willing to love. Jesus is punished as our substitute as the precondition for God's acceptance of us. For all its moral earnestness, this view is not worthy of the Gospel. The second approach ignores the importance of holiness, which gives depth to our understanding of

divine love and prevents it from being turned into a superficial in-
dulgence on God's part. The biblical witness is most adequately
captured and the realities of our experience most powerfully addressed if we hold the dimensions of holiness and love in continuing tension, recognizing their paradoxical unity in God. In doing
this we can understand the cross of Christ as expressing the *cost of
divine love,* embodying both judgment and grace.

The late Scottish theologian, Donald Baillie, cites an analogy in
human relationships which is helpful in grasping the point we are
making.[6] If I, in a moment of weakness, betray a very dear friend
and do him considerable harm, will he pass over it lightly without
calling me to account for this betrayal? If he were not a true friend
but rather shallow in his attitude toward me, he might either pass
over the matter for the sake of comfortable relations, or sever our
relationship completely. But if he cares for me deeply, he will not
be able to follow either of these alternatives. He will seek me out,
but the judgment that rightly falls on me for committing this act
will make it difficult for my friend to forgive. Not that he is slow
to forgive, but his honest concern for me prevents him from taking
the matter lightly.

Perhaps this analogy can help us understand at least one important dimension of the cross. It is an expression of the cost of forgiveness. There is conflict and struggle in the atonement, but it is
not resolved by an offering of satisfaction to God in one form
or another. It is an atonement borne by God himself, and because
he is a holy God, this atonement is costly. Thus the cross is an expression at the same time of the holiness and love of God, the
judgment and forgiveness of God. They meet at the cross and the
cross tells the world that our rebellion does not destroy our divinely-
given destiny. It tells the world that love is the greatest power in
the world because love is of God, and he has dealt with us in love
—not a shallow, sentimental, indulgent love but a suffering, stead-
fast love.

It is clear that for Christian faith, Jesus Christ makes all the
difference. It is often argued that one person cannot bear this
uniqueness, and that Christianity could better talk of Jesus' religion
instead of making a religion about Jesus. The former approach

would focus on Jesus the teacher, while the latter focuses on the person of Jesus as the embodiment of what he taught. Jesus spoke of God's love which reaches out to the lost (Luke 15), but the Christian community perceived the singular expression of God's love in his own life and his death on the cross. It is not simply his ideas that are important, but his identity to which he testified in word and deed. It is important to remember that this discussion of the atonement presupposes Jesus' resurrection. That which sealed the conviction of his followers that "God was in Christ" was his resurrection from the dead. This remains the ultimate mystery concerning Jesus, a mystery which points us to the destiny of the human family. In talking about Jesus we have thus been compelled to talk about God, and what we understand God to be has been informed by what we perceive to be the meaning of Jesus' life. It is time now to give further attention to the Christian understanding of God.

6

God–The Mystery

IN THIS CHAPTER WE ADDRESS the central subject of theology according to its literal meaning: the study of God. Some indication of the crisis in faith and theology today is seen in the fact that since the 1960s it has been common in theological circles to speak of the "problem of God," or the "loss of transcendence." These statements reflect the impact of secularism, that personal and cultural attitude which defines reality exclusively in terms of this world. It is a view of life that is one-dimensional, or what William Blake called "single vision." In the 1960s there were many theologians who became convinced that our culture was undergoing a profound and irreversible transition described as a process of secularization, and that Christianity, having contributed to that process in various ways, should not oppose it but adapt herself to it. That meant a reconsideration of the doctrine of God in which the traditional notion of transcendence would have to be overcome in behalf of an exclusively immanental view: God is not above or beyond us, but exclusively within our world.

This collapsing of divine transcendence was vigorously repudiated by a group of theologians who met at Hartford Theological Seminary in Hartford, Connecticut in January, 1975. They issued an appeal to all Christians—the "Hartford Appeal"—for a recovery of transcendence and a rejection of those prevailing assumptions of our society's intellectual establishment which are "false and debilitating to the Church's life and work." Some of those ideas we have discussed in referring to the challenges to Christian faith today (Chapter 1), but the Hartford Appeal identifies the crucial issue as a suffocating secularism which results in "a world without windows." The common-sense world has become a self-enclosed world, leaving us embarrassed to speak of the God who addresses us in the events of our lives and to whom we can pray.

In centuries past the believer had no difficulty in accepting the image of transcendence as a literal description of where God was —"up there" or "in heaven." This was imagery which fit in with the dominant conception of the universe, the common worldview. Today this is no longer the case, and the consequent rethinking of the doctrine of God has become particularly intense during our own times. Much attention has been given to the nature of theological language; new philosophical models have been adopted which provide new imagery and concepts with which to refer to God and express his relation to the world; and for some the hard conclusion has been drawn that Christianity can be affirmed without God, a kind of humanistic, Jesus-centered faith. In this chapter we shall affirm transcendence as indispensable to what Christians believe, while at the same time recognizing the need of Christians to understand the peculiar nature of the language they use in speaking of God. This need has become critical in a world which no longer feels at home with the language and imagery of traditional theism.

It should be clear from the previous chapters that the Christian stands in the midst of a tradition which celebrates and proclaims the reality of God on the basis of certain historical events. Our discussion of faith and revelation in the opening chapters necessarily involved reference to God, for revelation presupposes God as revealer. When we turned to the subject of human life and destiny we were also compelled to speak of God in order to fully understand and answer the question, "Who am I?" In addressing the Word of God, Jesus Christ, it was of course necessary once again to bring the subject of God into the discussion. Consequently, the outlines of a Christian understanding of God have by now already emerged. In discussing these other topics first, we have implicitly acknowledged that any discussion of God from a Christian viewpoint involves the human situation and our encounter with a historical revelation. But now we must examine more closely the Christian understanding of God and consider the problems which confront this understanding in today's world.

The Problem of God-Talk

Briefly stated, the problem of our talk about God is this: how can our language, which reflects the world of time and space, be used to describe God who is not in this world of time and space but who by definition is the author of this world? Or put in another way, how can finite language be used to talk about God who is infinite? Theologians have long been aware of the problem of theological language, but until recently most people sitting in the pew on a Sunday morning have not spent much time pondering the matter. They have been familiar with talk about God in the manner of the Bible, with no questions asked as to the nature of that language. But in our own times, significant numbers of laypeople are experiencing difficulties with the assumption that we are talking literally or descriptively about God. We shall examine briefly several categories which may help us in understanding the nature of God-language.

Theological Language as Myth, Analogy and Paradox

One category which is often used to describe language about God is *myth*. It is an exceedingly rich concept, with a variety of definitions. In our discussion of the fall we noted that theologians use the category of myth to denote this imaginative story which involves the interaction of God and humans, and which conveys a profound truth concerning the human situation. Many would associate myth exclusively with a primal age in which it describes those things which happened at the "beginning" of life as we know it, and which account for the structures of today. Myths are always stories and are always personal, but they are not intended to be understood as history. They describe archetypal events which are actually recurring patterns or realities of human life (Claude Levi-Strauss puts it simply and directly when he says that a "myth is a story that aims to explain why things are as they are"). The story of creation and the story of the fall would properly be called myths because they account for and interpret realities on the basis of what "happened" in the beginning of time. In this way the Christian tradition has expressed the truth that we are creatures of God and at the same time are not fulfilling the destiny for which he has created us.

One very influential view of myth in theological circles is that proposed by Rudolf Bultmann. He does not associate myth with a primal age but applies it to all the language in the Bible which describes God in relation to the world. He defines myth as "the use of imagery to express the otherworldly in terms of this world and the divine in terms of human life, the other side in terms of this side." [1] Bultmann has performed a service in sensitizing theologians to the symbolic character of talk about God, but there are implications in his understanding of myth which are open to question. He seems to regard it as a way of thinking which can be limited to ancient peoples who were not in the habit of thinking abstractly. He also identifies mythical language with a three-story universe consisting of heaven, earth and hell which is no longer plausible to a scientific age. The result is that myth for Bultmann is something to be cast aside as obsolete. We would argue that myth remains as a compelling story-form to express our sense of living in a world whose origin and destiny belong to God. The important thing, once again, is to understand the nature of the language we use.

Myth is but one form of symbolic language. *Symbol,* like myth, is a tremendously rich concept which is variously defined in different contexts. We can say that a word taken from everyday life and experience and used to illuminate the ultimate meaning or destiny of human life is functioning as a religious symbol. It is a concept which serves as a window to transcendent meaning. For example, within the Christian context the cross on which Jesus was nailed has become a symbol which conveys the event of Jesus' suffering and death as a redemptive act of God. As such the symbol is revelation to the believer, evoking faith and exercising the power to reorient and redirect one's life. As a particular form of symbolic discourse, myth provides a framework rooted in primordial time and within which the whole of life is understood. As such a myth invites our belief and is not a myth if it does not do so. In our discussion of the myth of the fall, we noted the insights brought to the human condition by means of that story, and we shall note the same in regard to the story of creation in the next chapter.

Another category which has played an important role in the understanding of theological language is *analogy*. The use of this concept assumes that our talk about God can in some way bridge the "distance" between God and ourselves and actually convey theoretical knowledge concerning God. This does not mean, however, that our language about God is literally descriptive, or univocal. If we understood words used to describe God in exactly the same way as words used in describing human beings or any object within the world, we would deny God's transcendence. God would become an idol. But it does not follow that the only alternative is to say that God-language is equivocal, or bears an entirely different meaning from that which we understand. This would deny the possibility of our saying anything for sure about God. The answer of theology has been to speak of analogy, meaning that personal terms descriptive of human beings can be applied to God in analogous fashion. Thus we can speak of God as loving or merciful or long-suffering, and be saying something meaningful in that the words can be understood as similar in meaning to those words used in the context of human relationships.

The question naturally arises, on what basis do theologians claim that analogy is an appropriate category to describe the meaning of theological language? Thomas Aquinas (c. 1225-1274), the theological patron saint of Roman Catholicism, refined the argument which has been identified with Catholic theology in answer to this question. It is called the "analogy of being" *(analogia entis)*, which is based on the concept of being taken from Greek philosophy and which expresses the unity and underlying reality of all that is. The difference between God and us is that God is pure being and the Source of all being, for whom it is inconceivable that he could "not be." We, on the other hand, are in the state of creaturely existence and thus subject to non-being—each of us shall die. Despite this difference, the unity between divine and human being enables us to speak of God in analogical language. This means that in spite of the divine mystery, we can at least make statements about God which are similar in meaning to statements about ourselves.

Protestant theologians today find little use in this argument. Their alternative is to root the possibility of our talking about God in the concept of revelation and the response of faith evoked by that revelation. We have noted the historical understanding of revelation in Christian faith, which means that God does not reveal himself directly in some kind of immediate encounter. If God is known in and through historical events, then he is known indirectly, and talk about God is rooted in things that have happened and which convey a revelatory message to the believer. Christian talk about God is thus inextricably tied up with the historical event of Jesus and the meaning of his life, death, and resurrection. The concept of analogy is still useful in this approach, but it is based not on the concept of being but on the Christian understanding of revelation. God discloses himself indirectly and therefore what we say about him involves a transfer of meaning from contexts within our life and history to God himself. It involves the conviction that if God reveals himself in human events, then human language is able to convey something truthful about God, in spite of the mystery.

A third category which is helpful in understanding God-talk is *paradox*. A paradox is commonly defined as an apparent contradiction, in which two statements stand in opposition to each other but are not really contradictory. They are capable of being resolved in a hidden unity which is not clear to us. We may say, "Mary is certainly a paradox," because we know her well enough to be puzzled over what she did yesterday. But we call her a paradox because we suspect that we could find a basis for her action if we knew all that there was to know about what she did and why she did it. In the case of Mary it is possible to resolve the paradox by discovering the "mystery" behind the situation we described. But when we speak of God, the mystery and thus the paradox are not capable of being removed.

Paradox has always been a part of religious discourse because it involves the "description" of God, who is indescribable. There is tension in every affirmation about God because it cannot simply be taken at face-value, as we have noted in our discussion of myth and analogy. We speak of God, and yet he eludes our speech. We seek to conceptualize or objectify him and we end up in contradictions because we then turn him into a finite being. The deepest paradox in Christian language concerning God is the affirmation that God is both transcendent and immanent, both mystery beyond our comprehension and the loving Presence proclaimed in the Gospel of Jesus Christ. We can also speak of the paradoxes inherent to Christian experience which are reflected in theological statements. At the center of that experience is the recognition that one is acceptable to God because of the undeserved goodness or grace of God. We are accountable before God in our freedom and at the same time we are wholly dependent on God. Divine grace and human freedom together form the paradox which marks the essential character of Christian experience.

God as Person

In the early 1960s a little book was published by the Anglican theologian and bishop, John A. T. Robinson, entitled *Honest to God*. As much as any one book, it articulated for many people the problems they were either vaguely or acutely experiencing in regard to their understanding of God. Robinson argues that supernaturalism, or the notion of God as a person who reigns over the world, is no longer a viable belief. He agrees with atheists who reject such an image, and he suspects that most atheists are anti-theists (opposed to this theistic view of God) rather than true atheists. In order to avoid trivializing the notion of transcendence, Robinson proposes another spatial metaphor, that of depth, to express what we mean by transcendence. Here he follows theologian Paul Tillich, who rejects the traditional language of theism because it turns God into a being beside others and consequently subjects God to the limitations of finitude. To speak of God as a person who encounters us is another way of making God finite for we objectify him and thus make him a part of the world. Tillich asserts that it is impossible to say that God exists, for existence is a characteristic of finite creatures. He proposes that we think of God as ground and depth of being—or being-itself—in order to get beyond the gods of human imagination. In an effort to transcend theism Tillich also speaks of "God above God" who is neither subject nor object, the "transpersonal presence of the divine." This is God who is the power of being-itself, the reality that is captured in a fragmentary way in the traditional symbols of the church.

These problems reflect the paradox we have noted in the Christian doctrine of God. Both personal and abstract language have contributed to the formation of the church's tradition, but the difficulty of uniting them effectively has always been a problem. The God of Aristotle is the Absolute or Pure Being; such concepts provided a satisfying answer to the philosophical problems which concerned the Greeks, but are inadequate to an understanding of a God who encounters human beings in historical events. At the same time, many theologians argue that ontological (from the Greek word for "being"), abstract language conveys a needed sense of ultimacy concerning God which is lost in personal language. In view of the difficulties of theistic language today, what should be the response of Christian theology? Should it abandon the personal, dramatic language of scripture in favor of a more philosophical, abstract image of God?

Both types of language have their appropriate use if we remember that the terms we use do not literally describe God. However, there is a fundamental assumption concerning God that the Christian would not want to deny. This assumption is that God is not less than personal, such as an impersonal force or a reality which cannot be addressed. If God were an "it" about which we could conceptualize and theorize, then God would be an idol of our own construction. The mystery and transcendence which we want to express in the concept of God necessarily involves our standing before a Presence, a "Thou" before whom we gain a sense of our creaturehood and dependence. In other words, to speak of God in a Christian sense is to speak of a *relationship* to God which illumines our own existence, and this relationship involves the necessity of personal language concerning God. This does not mean, however, that we can conclude that God is *a* person who can be described in any objective sense. God is the word we use to apply to the mystery which defines us, and to do justice to that mystery

we use personal language. We may be inclined at times to speak
of God as "ground of being," but he is the same God who addresses
us in the story of our lives.

We have several times noted that Jesus called God "Father,"
which is certainly the most commonly used personal term in Christian language concerning God. The word raises a problem today,
however, in view of the women's movement. Can we continue to
use such an explicitly masculine word as "Father" when speaking
of God? There is no doubt that theology has been excessively masculine in the past, and a masculine-paternal framework in Christianity has had an obvious impact in subordinating women in the
church. However, the problem is compounded if we substitute the
word "Mother" for "Father" when speaking of God. Nor does it
appear feasible to call God "Parent," as some suggest. What must
be stressed is that God transcends sexuality. Language used in
speaking of God has appropriately included characteristics which
could be regarded as maternal as well as paternal; the God of power
is the God of care, comfort and compassion. Sex itself is not the
issue. The issue is whether the God of care and compassion will
prevail in every aspect of the church's life and mission.[2]

The use of personal language in speaking of God is often described as anthropomorphism, or speaking of God as an exalted
human being. However, our point is not that we are describing
God, which would leave us with a god or idol of our own making.
We are instead confessing that the most adequate way to speak of
God is by using personal, dialogic language, which recognizes that
we are being addressed by God in the circumstances and relationships of life. The revelation of God in Christ brings the personal
presence of God into the experience of being held to account in the
moral life, being forgiven and restored to a sense of integrity, and
being turned to the future with a sense of trust and confidence,
even in the face of death. To recognize the personal reality of God
in these experiences is to give one's life a perspective that illumines
what it means to be human.

The claim that a personal God is simply a projection of human
personality has been countered by theologians with the question
whether the ideal of personhood is not derived from religious

experience, or our being addressed by God. How can the infinite worth of human personality be affirmed unless there is an infinite being to whom we are valuable, and by whom we evaluate human personhood? In other words, our personhood, which is not always self-evident to us as we persist in treating each other as objects rather than as persons, actually receives its unique inviolability because we are children of God and have been brought to an awareness of that fact.

One incomparably rich concept in Christian theology that has been used to unite the dimensions of both person and mystery in our thinking about God is *spirit*. When applied to ourselves the concept of spirit denotes our essential personhood as willing, reasoning, intentional beings. As spirit we are created in God's image and capable of responding to the divine presence, but as creatures our spirit-nature is dependent upon God as spirit. Thus the concept of spirit conveys the personal reality of God without imposing the limitations of human spirit. Spirit also conveys the presence and mystery of divine being that is beyond human comprehension. It expresses transcendence, not in the sense of God being totally removed in a distant realm but in the sense that God as spirit is not subject to our grasp or manipulation. This truth, as we noted above, also expresses the personal reality of God who is not an "it" to be manipulated but a "Thou" in whose presence the only appropriate response is that of worship. In expressing both the personal reality and the mystery of God, spirit does not define (limit) God but would place God beyond our capacity to define.

Our Knowledge of God

Two points in particular have been made thus far which are relevant to consideration of our knowledge of God. We have noted, first, the importance of the concept of revelation to Christian experience and belief. To speak of God is necessarily to speak of Jesus Christ, in whom God is known. We have noted, further, that knowledge of God is not a theoretical matter which one could keep at arm's length. It is existential knowledge, or knowledge which reflects a new self-understanding in light of one's knowledge of God. It is a testimony, one might say, to one's having been known by God.

These observations would appear to contradict attempts made by various theologians and philosophers to arrive at God by another route than revelation. Their arguments have been regarded in the past as proofs for the existence of God, bearing a rationality which could not be doubted by the open-minded person. Today few theologians would want to speak of "proofs" for God's existence, but most would acknowledge not only the possibility but the necessity of citing evidences from one's consideration of the world or from some aspect of human experience that at least point to the possibility of God. We shall note briefly a few of the more celebrated arguments.

Arguments for the Reality of God

One of the most distinctive and celebrated attempts to prove the existence of God is the ontological argument of Anselm, based on the notion of God itself. He begins by claiming that we possess an idea of "the most perfect and real conceivable being." This is an a priori idea, which means it is inherent to the human mind and not learned from experience. Such a being must and therefore does exist, because a nonexistent being could not be the most perfect and real conceivable being. In short, the very idea of God necessitates the reality of God. Objections to this argument were not long in coming; a monk by the name of Gaunilo asked Anselm whether his idea of a perfect island meant that the island must exist. Anselm's response shows that his statement can be applied meaningfully only to that being which is uncreated, or God. In other words, the very concept of divine being logically includes his existence, or reality.

Thomas Aquinas was also not satisfied with Anselm's argument. He looked for evidence of God's existence in the world around him, and found there the effects of a divine First Cause. Coming from Aristotle, Aquinas argues that the world is inherently unintelligible if we do not posit an ultimate Source for it. Everything in nature points beyond itself for its sufficient explanation, and we either end up with an infinite regress in which nothing is finally explained, or we must conclude that there is an ultimate being which is self-sufficient or self-existent, needing nothing else to account for its existence. Such a being is what we mean by God. Another argument of Aquinas is based on the fact that we live in a cosmos rather than in chaos. The design and order of the universe leads us necessarily to the conclusion that a supreme Intelligence has created and ordered it. This is the cosmological argument, which was often argued in various forms during the period of the Enlightenment.

Immanuel Kant (1724-1804) represents a turning point in the history of these arguments. In his *Critique of Pure Reason* he maintains that all attempts on the part of philosophers to arrive at God on the basis of logical argument are doomed to failure. They either contain the necessity of existence within their definition of God (the ontological argument) and thus beg the question, or the evidence from the world used to argue the existence of God can be easily countered with evidence which leads one to conclude that there is no God. Our reason simply cannot demonstrate any truth which pertains to a realm beyond the world we experience. Kant's conclusions profoundly influenced much of the theology of Protestantism, which during the nineteenth and twentieth centuries has tended to be skeptical of metaphysics, or theorizing about God apart from revelation. Yet Kant, the son of a clergyman, found another way to God apart from what he called "theoretical reason." That way was through our "practical reason," or the moral consciousness. God, he argues, is a postulate of our moral experience, for the duty to pursue the highest good presupposes a God of intelligence and will who corresponds to our own moral character and who has ordered the world according to the moral law. For Kant, the experience of moral duty is the one convincing argument for the existence of God.

A theologian whose work reflects the emerging Romanticist reaction to the Enlightenment, Friedrich Schleiermacher (1768-1834), provides another avenue to the reality of God. He does not intend it as a proof of God's existence, but is concerned to demonstrate to those he calls "the cultured despisers of religion" that if they plumb the depths of their own personal experience, they will become aware of their relation to God. He delineates this relation in terms of a feeling of absolute dependence. It is not a specific feeling or emotion as such, and it is not a direct apprehension of God himself, but a fundamental underlying sense of dependence which provides the basis for people talking about God. Schleiermacher is not referring to a mystical encounter with an infinite being, but understands this feeling of absolute dependence as occasioned by our experience of the totality of the natural world. The infinite is experienced solely in and through the finite. This strong experiential thrust in Schleiermacher carried with it a relational understanding of God: we cannot speak of God as he is in himself, but only in terms of our experience of God as finite creatures, within the limits of the world in which we live.

A notable twentieth century attempt to establish and clarify our apprehension of God is that of Rudolf Otto in his book, *The Idea of the Holy*. Reflecting the influence of Schleiermacher a century earlier, he also directs our attention to the depths of human awareness in order to speak of God. What he discerns in deeply-felt religious experience—though not always awakened in everyone—is a sense of the "numinous," or of the holy. It is an apprehension which provides the core of religious experience, a unique awareness which cannot be explained in terms of a moral sense, nor as a feeling of absolute dependence. While Schleiermacher described the sense of dependence as primary, from which one arrives at God as the One on whom we are dependent, Otto maintains an immediate sense of the holy as a reality outside of oneself. The name he gives to this reality is the *mysterium tremendum,* or "aweful mystery," exciting a sense of majesty, awe and power. The mystery is perceived as "wholly other," and yet as immediate and overpowering. A quote from Otto gives us something of the flavor of his argument:

> . . . we are dealing with something for which there is only one appropriate expression, *"mysterium tremendum."* The feeling of it may at times come sweeping like a gentle tide, pervading the mind with a tranquil mood of deepest worship. It may pass over into a more set and lasting attitude

of the soul, continuing, as it were, thrillingly vibrant and resonant, until at last it dies away and the soul resumes its "profane," non-religious mood of everyday experience. It may burst in sudden eruption up from the depths of the soul with spasms and convulsions, or lead to the strangest excitements, to intoxicated frenzy, to transport, and to ecstasy. It has its wild and demonic forms and can sink to an almost grisly horror and shuddering. It has its crude, barbaric antecedents and early manifestations, and again it may be developed into something beautiful and pure and glorious. It may become the hushed, trembling, and speechless humility of the creature in the presence of—whom or what? In the presence of that which is a mystery inexpressible and above all creatures.[3]

These words remind one of the speech of a mystic, but Otto is critical of mysticism, claiming it is too non-rational and leads to such an excessive creature-consciousness that the self is in danger of being annihilated or totally absorbed in the infinite.

We have considered a number of arguments which seek to establish the existence or reality of God. Each one of them has found its supporters within the Christian community, and in the case of some of them a tremendously rich and varied literature has resulted from the continuing debate over their meaning and validity. How shall we evaluate these arguments? Is any one of them likely to carry weight for the person who does not believe in God? Are they important to the person who does believe in God? What kind of knowledge are they dealing with, and what is its relation to the knowledge of God we discussed in Chapter 2 in connection with revelation? These are questions which have occasioned considerable debate in Christian theology, and they ask for an answer from us as well.

Natural Theology and Revelation

Natural theology refers to attempts to arrive at God apart from faith or without appealing to a special revelation. These attempts are philosophical arguments, making an appeal to our reason or

some aspect of our experience. The arguments we have just considered are examples of natural theology, for they proceed from
evidences of one kind or another which supposedly lead to God,
whether it be from the idea of God we have in our minds, the
order and purpose inherent to the natural world, the experience of
moral obligation, the feeling of absolute dependence, or the sense
of the holy. A perennial question in Christian theology is how to
relate natural theology to revelation theology, or reflection which is
based on the historical revelation to which the scriptures witness.
One obvious way to relate the two is to find them complementary
to each other. Historically this has been the Roman Catholic position, in which it is argued that in virtue of our reason we can
arrive at the conclusion that there is a God who is benevolent.
However, this knowledge is limited since there are certain supernatural truths concerning God which one can know only through
revelation. The dogma of the Trinity is then cited as an example
of this.

Protestant theology, on the other hand, has been more suspicious
of attempts to arrive at God apart from revelation. The reformers
agreed that in principle we can know God, but in reality since we
are living in the fallen state of sinfulness, we cannot arrive at
knowledge of God apart from divine grace. A common solution in
Protestant theology has been to distinguish between "general" and
"special" revelation, in which the former refers to a revelation of
God in the world of nature and human experience to the point
that our responsibility before God is established (cf. Rom. 1-2). It
is a recognition that human beings are religious and respond to
God in a variety of ways, however distorted or inadequate from a
Christian viewpoint. Jesus Christ as God's good news is then designated as "special" or "saving" revelation, in virtue of it being the
Word of God that has entered into our history as a peculiar act of
divine grace. This distinction between general and special revelation
was vigorously attacked by Karl Barth, founder of the neo-orthodox
school which dominated Protestant theology from 1930 through
the 1950s. Barth became convinced that natural theology (or general revelation) has imported ideas about God which are not only
foreign to the God of biblical revelation, but actually subvert that

revelation. His answer was to develop a Christocentric theology which stressed the *exclusive* revelation of God in Jesus Christ. According to Barth, there is absolutely no knowledge of God worthy of the name apart from Christ. He constitutes the Gospel, God's "Yes!" to the human race which is found nowhere else.

As one might expect, each of these responses to natural theology has its particular strengths as well as its weaknesses. Those who evaluate natural theology positively are usually impressed with the universality of religious consciousness, and see it as the necessary assumption to the possibility of revelation as it is understood by Christians. If there were no awareness of God, then the revelation in Christ as the Word of God would have no possibility of being understood for what it is.[4] On the other hand, is there any relation between the God of natural theology and the God of biblical revelation? There are those who argue that natural theology leads us to the Void, a threatening Mystery without a name. Others ask whether we can really find God at the end of an argument. Such a "God," if proved, is no more than an idea, neither relevant nor helpful to either the believer or the unbeliever. The distinctiveness of the Christian understanding of God is that through the revelation in Christ, he is given a name. God becomes the Father of our Lord Jesus Christ. He is not an idea at the end of an argument, but the personal reality behind the life, death and resurrection of Jesus.

In recent years the work of Paul Tillich has been particularly significant in recasting the discussion of natural theology. In his method of correlation, he sees the human condition giving rise to questions concerning the meaning of human existence, questions which press at the boundaries of our knowledge and demand answers. They are the fundamental questions which concern us in these pages—Who am I? Is there a God? What difference does it make for me? What is life's destiny? Tillich then poses the revelation in Jesus Christ as the answer which speaks to these questions. In this theological method, natural theology is understood as raising the important questions, but not providing the ultimate answers.[5] The questions reveal our nature as inquiring beings whose lives are directed to an ultimate end beyond ourselves. The proofs for God's existence embody these questions, but they also reflect the convictions of faith already present in the argument. Proofs for God's existence are intended to be based on grounds which are evident to every open, fair-minded person, and as such they are exercises in the philosophy of religion. But philosophy brings us to the boundary lines of thought in its speculation concerning God; if it goes beyond to claim God as the end of its argument, it must be in virtue of a "leap" of faith. To say that there are human experiences which raise the possibility of God is one thing; to say there are human experiences which bring us inevitably to the conclusion that God *is,* is something else. The former is natural theology, or philosophy concerning itself with the subject of religion; the latter is the expression of religious faith itself.

The arguments of natural theology can be appreciated, then, as another indication among many in human life for considering the *possibility* of God. The fact that God is a question that people are driven to is important in itself. From the viewpoint of faith, it is an indication of the reality of God that people are animated by the question of his existence. These arguments also point to the fact that faith in God does not occur in a vacuum. Faith arises where human beings become concerned with matters that are essential to their humanity, matters which we have been addressing in the preceding chapters. These fundamental, human concerns cannot be regarded as proofs for God's existence, but they can be seen as reasons of the heart which contribute to one's taking the leap of faith. Let's review them briefly.

In Chapter 1 we noted that human beings seek a meaning and purpose to life, and this desire leads to fundamental convictions about who we are and why we are here. These convictions reach ultimately to the possibility of God as the Source and End of life, providing us with both an anchor and a sense of direction. We noted further in Chapter 3 that we human beings, in spite of our promise, are also a problem to ourselves. We experience conflict between good intentions and the temptations of evil, a struggle which threatens our identity and which can lead us to remorse and even despair. We yearn for wholeness, a sense of personal integration which enables us to live effectively and to be at peace with ourselves and our neighbors. This quest for wholeness and healing turns us to the possibility of God as the Source of forgiveness and reconciliation. We noted also that we human beings struggle against limitations of many kinds, the most threatening and final of which is death. Our mortality stamps itself indelibly upon our total experience as human beings. We are creatures of hope who look to the future as promise, and yet the future also confronts us as the threat of nothingness. To speak of God in the face of death is thus to affirm our future and consequently affirm the meaningfulness of our past and present as well.

It is clear from these considerations that why a person believes in God is very much an existential matter, involving the question of one's existence as a vulnerable, incomplete, searching, hoping, often self-destructive and thoroughly mortal creature. Paul Tillich has put it well when he characterized human life as a question which seeks an answer, or we could say a quest which seeks fulfillment. For the Christian that quest is answered in the God of the cross and resurrection.

There is no doubt that human nature is capable of producing its own gods as answers to the questions and needs we have just been discussing. People are prodigious idol-makers, and they do it also in the name of religion. Unfortunately, the history of the Christian church itself provides ample testimony to our inclination to manipulate the idea of God for our own purposes. The Christian experience of revelation, however, puts this selfish use of religion under radical judgment. The God who is Father of our Lord Jesus Christ challenges us to radical conversion in light of the cross of Christ and what it means for human behavior. Here we come to the essential meaning of revelation as it is perceived in Christian faith, over against all attempts to arrive at God apart from that revelation. The revelation in Christ does not simply give us additional information about God, but bestows a new orientation to life that is shaped by the cross and resurrection. When the life of Jesus Christ becomes to us the Word of God, or revelation, then his cross and resurrection become our own dying-to-self and finding new life in Christ. Revelation is thus the occasion of repentance and renewal. When the Christian speaks of God, he speaks of these realities within the context of the ultimate meaning and destiny of human life.

This understanding of revelation recognizes its antithetical, critical character. In Christ, God comes to us in judgment as well as in grace, destroying our pretensions and false expectations as well as showing us a better way. Paul expresses this truth quite forcefully:

> Where is the wise man? Where is the scribe? Where is the debater of this age? Has not God made foolish the wisdom of the world? For since in the wisdom of God, the world did not know God through wisdom, it pleased God through the folly of what we preach to save those who believe. For Jews demand signs and Greeks seek wisdom, but we preach Christ crucified, a stumbling block to Jews and folly to Gentiles, but to those who are called, both Jews and Greeks, Christ the power of God and the wisdom of God. For the foolishness of God is wiser than men, and the weakness of God is stronger than men (1 Cor. 1:20-25).

At the beginning of the modern era, it was Martin Luther who developed Paul's insights concerning revelation in his "theology of the cross" *(theologia crucis)*. Luther delighted in contrasting the knowledge of God through the suffering Christ on the cross with the knowledge that is based on the works of creation. The former knowledge humbles and cleanses the repentant heart, thus restoring our true humanity. The latter knowledge, however, leaves us believing in our own integrity and consequently our knowledge of God is used to establish ourselves and our own causes—in short, to deify ourselves. Luther saw this happening in the "theology of glory" *(theologia gloriae)* which characterized the teaching of the medieval church. The result was to exalt the church without acknowledging that God's judgment begins with the church, or those who perceive the meaning of the cross.

We noted above that the revelation of God according to Christian understanding is indirect. The cross and resurrection are God's ways of encountering human beings, but the presence of God in these events is not apparent to everyone who considers them. Furthermore, to those who have been addressed in these events, there is no removal of the veil between God and themselves which would enable them to walk by sight, rather than by faith. This leads us to observe that even in revelation, God remains hidden. If God were not hidden, he would not be God because then he would be fully comprehensible. This fact led Pascal to observe, "Every religion that does not affirm that God is hidden is not true." There is no way of making God obvious to anyone, nor is there any way of certifying or proving his reality among those who believe in him. The significance of the Christian revelation is that it gives the mystery of God a name: "Father of our Lord Jesus Christ." This means that God is no longer sheer mystery for the Christian, a word that compels silence or despair. The mystery now for Christians is that they know they cannot fully understand or fathom the miracle of divine love.

The Dogma of the Trinity

Through the centuries Christians have regarded the Trinitarian dogma with fascination and puzzlement. Many non-Christians have written it off as one more absurdity among others to be found in the Christian church. What is the meaning and significance of this dogma? The adjective form of trinity, "triune," expresses more clearly the meaning of the word as the unity of three and one. As such the dogma of the Trinity, or the "Blessed Trinity" in the language of many Christians, affirms the distinctly Christian understanding of God as Father, Son, and Holy Spirit. This threefold reference to God arose as a result of Jesus Christ and the meaning he assumed for the church as resurrected Lord. It was basically a Christological problem in deciding how to relate Jesus to God the Father. By taking Jesus seriously as revelation of God, the church was drawn to binitarian (two in one) language and ultimately to trinitarian language as the experience of God's presence was expressed in the concept of Spirit.

The formulation of the Trinity as a doctrine is not found in the New Testament. It was hammered out during the fourth century in what is called the Trinitarian controversy. The church was attempting to take the New Testament language of Father, Son, and Holy Spirit with absolute seriousness, basing its doctrine of God on the historical revelation to which scripture witnesses. Using the philosophical language of the Hellenistic world, the term for essence or substance (Latin: *substantia*) was used to convey the transcendent reality and unity of God, while the term *persona* was used to convey the three-fold character of God as Father, Son, and Spirit. The term, *persona* did not convey the notion of an individual center of self-consciousness as does our word, "person." The word was used in drama to designate the mask worn by players as they assumed the role of different characters. As the word took on the meaning of person as we know it, the danger of tritheism, or belief in three gods, became all the more apparent. It is this sense of three individual persons which has made the doctrine such a mathematical puzzle in reconciling three with one.[6]

Theologians often seek to emphasize that the Trinity is not a departure from monotheism, and to safeguard the unity of our conception of God it has been suggested by Karl Barth and others that we do not use the word "person" but "modes of being" or similar expressions. This would more accurately convey the meaning of the ancient church in using *persona*. But if theologians are concerned about the unity of God, it is probably just as true that devotional literature and practice continue to emphasize the distinct and separate persons of the Godhead. It is not uncommon for God the Father to be characterized as the stern judge, and Jesus the loving son. The story is told of one Christian group which prayed to each of the three persons in succession, until an answer to their problem was found!

In current theology there are two tendencies in the way in which the Trinity is addressed. On the one hand it is regarded as a theological construction which is not essential to expressing the Christian faith; it reflects the church's attempt to harmonize the New Testament language with monotheism and also defends that language against attacks from non-Christian sources. The other view has been most vigorously asserted by Karl Barth. He maintains that the Trinitarian dogma, while it is admittedly a theological construction several centuries later than the New Testament, is nonetheless directly derived from the New Testament and expresses the very heart and essence of the Christian revelation. As such it stands for Barth as the means of defending the revelation in Jesus Christ against proponents of natural theology both within and outside the church whose views of God are derived from sources other than scripture itself.

It should be stressed that this dogma is an attempt to take seriously the New Testament revelation and Christian experience which has been shaped by that revelation. When the New Testament speaks of God as Father, Son, and Spirit, the church responds by affirming in the dogma of the Trinity that God really *is* as he has revealed himself to be. Thus it is an affirmation of faith, but it is admittedly true that it has proved the vehicle for much questionable speculation on the part of theologians who have dwelt at length on the inner relations of the Trinity. Here one must remind oneself of the nature of theological language. Christian faith affirms with the Trinity that God really *is* the creating, reconciling and renewing God expressed in Father, Son and Spirit, without pretending that the doctrine is a blueprint description of God as he is in himself. Nor is the language of the fourth century dogma to be regarded as sacred and absolute. But through the centuries it has served the church well in keeping it faithful to the God revealed in the life, death and resurrection of Jesus Christ.

7

God and the World

THE APOSTLES' CREED BEGINS with the words, "I believe in God the Father Almighty, Maker of heaven and earth" (the First Article). This statement of belief in God as creator immediately gives rise to thoughts of the transcendent power, majesty, and sovereignty of God. It is this image of God which leads theologians to use the more abstract language concerning God as Absolute, or ground of being, for the very magnitude of the image is difficult to unite with the personal language which Christians use. The image of creator has resulted in a list of divine attributes such as the omnipotence (he is all-powerful) and omniscience (he is all-knowing) of God, his eternity and his holiness, which sets him apart from all created existence. Theologians speak of the aseity of God, meaning that his existence is not derived from another source as in the case of us creatures, but is derived from himself alone. He is unconditional, self-sufficient. Such language impresses us as unduly abstract and theoretical, but its value is in asserting both the mystery and reality of God whose being is beyond our capability of grasping.

At the same time we must express the paradox in God's relation to the world: he is immanent as well as transcendent, *in* the world as well as *over against* the world. Christian theology has zealously resisted the temptation to remove this paradox, which occurs whenever one asserts either the exclusive transcendence or the exclusive immanence of God. This is the path taken by deism and pantheism, respectively. Deism, a term which comes from eighteenth century England, maintains God's transcendence as creator but finds no evidence for affirming his immanence or presence to the world.

God has withdrawn and the world is operating according to its own natural laws. Pantheism in contrast, maintains that God and nature are identical. Believing that there is only one reality or being, the pantheist regards everything in the world as a mode or appearance of God. Both deism and pantheism have their own implications for one's understanding of the world in which we live. The Christian view of God's transcendence and immanence bears its distinctive implications as well, which we shall elaborate in the following pages.

The World as Created

The meaning and importance of the Christian doctrine of creation is not that it provides an answer to how the world came into being, but that it gives to Christians a certain perspective on their lives and the world in which they live. It is a doctrine that is misused if it is regarded as empirical or scientific knowledge about the origin of the world. It is the language of faith, affirming that we human beings are creatures who live in a creation, an assertion which has profound meaning for our existence. It provides an orientation to the natural world in which we live and the role of the human family within that world. And of course it affirms the sovereignty of the creator and the dependence of us who are creatures.

Langdon Gilkey, in his book, *Maker of Heaven and Earth,*[1] points to several implications of our creatureliness. For one thing, it means that the world is endowed with a purpose and intelligibility which we may not always be able to discern. The meaningfulness of created life is not finally bestowed by ourselves but by our creator. Contrary to what the atheistic existentialist maintains, we are not in the midst of a vast, irrational universe, forced to create our own little circle of meaning within it. That would make our lives essentially tragic, as Camus and others have argued. But to affirm the world as creation and ourselves as creatures is to acknowledge a meaning and destiny to the world which we ourselves are not capable of giving it, and which we are not always willing or able to perceive.

Our creaturehood also brings home the reality of our dependence. All of creation is finite and derived, receiving its being ultimately from the creator. As creatures our existence is not necessary nor self-sufficient, but fortuitous and dependent on many factors over which we have no control. As such we are not immortal but transient, here for a while and gone tomorrow. Isaac Watts has strikingly pictured this character of our existence in his well-known hymn based on Psalm 90:

> Time, like an ever-rolling stream,
> Bears all its sons away;
> They fly forgotten, as a dream
> Dies at the opening day.

The pathos of our existence thus portrayed is then contrasted with the knowledge of God who transcends the transiency of our lives:

> O God, our help in ages past,
> Our hope for years to come,
> Be thou our guide while troubles last,
> And our eternal home!

This radical dependence and mortality of all creaturely life reminds Christians that nothing in creation is worthy of their absolute trust and devotion. Such devotion to another person or aspect of the creation is a form of idolatry. We tend to worship the expression of sublime beauty or awesome power, but nothing in creation is worthy of our worship. To know our creatureliness is to defend ourselves against the tendency to absolutize human achievements and to find in them the source of meaning for our lives. It is thus a bulwark against idolatry which denies the finite, transitory character of creation.

Just as important as these negative expressions concerning the finitude of creation is the positive affirmation that the creation is good! The doctrine of creation makes God responsible for the world, and consequently there is nothing in creation which is to be rejected as intrinsically evil. Christian faith opposes the view that the world of matter is evil in contrast to the spiritual realm, or that finite existence as such is evil and must be escaped by spiritual exercises in which one's spirit is united with the Infinite Spirit. To say that we are created in the image of God is to affirm the possibility of fulfillment in our lives in spite of our contingent, mortal existence. The Christian conviction of the goodness of creation has given Western culture a profound optimism concerning the human and natural world. It has helped to create the cultural environment which encouraged the rise of science and technology as an expression of human autonomy over the world.

We cannot speak of Western technology without recognizing another implication of the doctrine of creation which has become increasingly clear in recent years. In the biblical story of creation the special status of human beings is expressed in the statement that they shall have dominion over the world (Gen. 1:26). The history of this dominion, however, has become the story of human rapacity in exploiting the earth's resources. While we have created a formidable civilization, we have also exercised our dominion as though we were no longer the dependent creatures that we are, whose dependence is directly related to the resources of the earth. The creation story qualifies our dominion by placing us in a position of responsibility, or stewardship, to God. But unfortunately this side of our situation has too often been overlooked. Now in a world of diminishing resources we are being forced to recognize our responsibility as creatures in a creation which has been entrusted to us.

We have noted several personal or existential implications of the doctrine of creation and we have expressly stated that it is in this realm that discussion of the doctrine belongs. But you may well ask, doesn't creation have to do with the origin of the empirical world? And doesn't the Bible give us an account of creation which has been argued over the centuries against scientific theories of the world's origin? Isn't there a real issue here that involves religion vs. science? Our discussion above concerning theological language included references to the creation story as an example of myth. What does this mean for the centuries-long argument on this topic?

In order to correctly understand the biblical story of creation we must be clear about the question the story is answering. Old Testament scholarship tells us that stories like the creation and the fall are etiological, i.e., they answer the question of origins: Where did the world come from? How did things get this way? Why has our race made a mess of things? These questions arise from human reflection on the mysteries of life, and the answers given to them are basically religious answers expressed in the form of myth. But the answer in regard to creation is not simply religious; it is also scientific in the sense that it involves ideas about how the world came into being which were in accord with the primitive science of ancient times. In other words, there was no separation of religious affirmation from scientific knowledge. In the modern era this is no longer possible because the function of the language of science has become clearly distinguished from that of religious language. We know that what science addresses are the *how* questions, questions which arise from the world in which we live and ask for answers which empirical investigation should be able to provide. Religious questions are of a different sort, asking *why* the world came into being, or raising the question of a meaning and destiny to the world which cannot be conclusively answered on the basis of scientific evidence.

This difference between science and religion is reflected in the fact that science is interested in the question of the world's *origin,* while religion, professing faith in God, speaks of the *creation* of the world. Creation presupposes a creator, or God, while science cannot speak of God because God is not an acceptable hypothesis to scientific investigation.[2] There are several theories found among scientists concerning the origin of the world, and Christians who are also scientists will come to their conclusion on this matter on the basis of the scientific evidence available. It is not a religious question as such because all these theories presuppose the presence of matter in some form and do not raise the question why there is matter in the first place.[3] This latter question is philosophical or religious in character because it raises the issue of purpose, or the "why" of existence. Scientists who are also Christians will respond to such a question on the basis of their Christian convictions, for there is no scientific answer to that question.

This separation of the question of creation as the religious question of the meaning and purpose of human existence, over against the scientific question of origins, is a position commonly found among theologians today. However we still see Christians attempting to harmonize the creation story in Genesis[4] with bits and pieces of scientific knowledge. For example, it is suggested that the days of creation are meant to be aeons of time in order to harmonize the creation story with the scientific evidence that evolution has occurred over millions of years. Or great significance is placed on the order given for the creation of different species in line with what we know concerning the evolution of species. All such attempts are based on the mistaken assumption that the story in Genesis is a literal description of what took place, or in other words, the language of science. We noted above that the literary genre of the creation story is myth, expressing a profound affirmation concerning the meaning of life as created. As such, creation is not a moment (or many aeons) in time but a belief concerning the nature of our lives—we are creatures accountable to God.

There have been numerous attempts to construct views of creation which provide an answer to the question of how the world came into being, some of them based on pagan myths and Gnostic cosmologies. For example, there is the analogy of generation which pictures the world flowing forth from God like rays from the sun. Most familiar to people today is undoubtedly the model of a manufacturer, in which God makes or constructs the world out of matter. In the nineteenth and twentieth centuries a more sophisticated image has been based on the theory of evolution. In this view God is regarded as an indwelling Spirit or Life Force, acting as a creative power in the world. Such a view of creation does not restrict it to an event in the past, but sees it as a vital process which never stops. Teilhard de Chardin most recently has given a teleological or goal-directed character to this creative process, envisioning his Omega Point as the culmination which embraces both the natural world and human society.

Our own emphasis on the meaning of creation as the affirmation of God's sovereignty, our own creatureliness, and the intelligibility of our existence, leads us to avoid theorizing about the mode of God's creative activity. The important thing in the Christian understanding is the double affirmation of the transcendence and im-

manence of God, which means that God can neither be identified
with the world (pantheism) nor divorced from the world (deism).
It is not possible for us to fathom the immanence of God in relation to the natural world, and every attempt to do so will result
in speculation. We ourselves stand between God and the creation
at the same time as we are a part of creation. The meaningfulness
of the doctrine of creation is not to be found in speculating about
God and nature but in seeing ourselves as God's creatures in a
world which has been entrusted to us. We can regard the Christian idea of *creatio ex nihilo* (creation out of nothing) as the expression of the mystery of creation and the impossibility of our
grasping the creative work of God. The very notion of creation by
God is a paradox which defies any form of explanation that we
might give it.

These observations do not mean, however, that the world of nature is of no particular interest to Christian theology. In fact in
the Old Testament, the God of Israel is the God of history. His
Word of promise to his people entails judgment of the gods of
nature whom they were often tempted to worship. Nature is appreciated as God's creation, but when the Psalmist reflects on the
wonders of nature, he sees the God of the covenant. The same
focus on history is true of the New Testament as well, but there
are also passages which bring creation and history together and
prevent us from making the mistake of isolating the human story
from the environment in which it takes place. John 1, Colossians
1, and Hebrews 1 relate the redemptive work of Christ to the whole
of creation so that what is anticipated in the final consummation
is a "new creation" which fulfills both nature and history. Just what
this means is not comprehensible, but it recognizes the continuity
and the ultimate unity in destiny of both nature and history. If
history is meaningful, then the larger environment in which that
history takes place makes its own contribution to the meaning of
human life and cannot be divorced from it. Both God the creator
and God the redeemer bring history and nature together, with the
fulfillment of the one necessarily including the fulfillment of the
other.

Before leaving the subject of creation we note a fact which has raised serious doubts in modern times concerning the possibility of any meaning or purpose to this world in which we live or to the meaningfulness of human life. It is the unbelievable vastness of our universe, a fact which has considerable impact on our emotions as well as our intellect. Our telescopes have penetrated to distances of 5,000,000,000 light years, and we know that our sun is simply a small star in a typical galaxy. Such knowledge boggles the mind and makes us ask, "Are we really of any significance?" In thinking about this, we must recognize that size in itself is not the determiner of value or significance. What Jesus said about the sparrows tells us something about the importance of ourselves in a vast universe. It does not make us any less real, or deny the inherent value to human life. To the Christian the vastness of the universe provides yet a further dimension to his awe before the incomprehensible mystery of God the creator. The very awesomeness of that mystery may well console us, for the God of such a universe must be able to be present to every dimension of his creation (including possibly life on planets of other galaxies). The limitations of our earthbound imagination get in the way of our being able to appreciate all that may be involved in speaking of the transcendence and immanence of God!

Divine Sovereignty and Human Freedom

To say that God is creator is also to say that God is sovereign. This is a notion that conveys great comfort to the believer, but it has occasioned considerable questioning and anguish as well. To the unbeliever it has often caused defiance, as in the case of the nineteenth century philosopher, Friedrich Nietzsche, who railed against a despotic God who he believed must "die" in order for human beings to live. What do we mean when we say that God is sovereign? Is the sovereignty of God a threat to human freedom? In Chapter 3 we noted that freedom is essential to our very being, but non-Christians often question whether that freedom can be reconciled with belief in the sovereignty of a Supreme Being. They picture a sovereign God as holding us on puppet strings, otherwise God would not be truly sovereign. Or they speak of a

divine omniscience which must imply knowledge of the future
and the consequent conclusion that our future actions are already
determined.

The problem with this accusation is that it is based on a model
of the divine-human relationship which is not true to the Christian
understanding of God. Our ideas of God's sovereignty must be
shaped by the revelation in Christ, which means a sovereignty of
divine love. To say that "God is love" is to affirm, among other
things, that God's sovereign will is the realization of our humanity.
His sovereignty and our self-realization cannot be divorced from
each other because our destiny as his creatures is God himself. This
fact is uniquely portrayed in our own history in the person of Jesus.
He is the one among us in whom the sovereignty of God was realized. Because we are creatures of destiny, God's sovereignty is best
expressed in terms of our future. That future transcends our destiny
as mortal creatures precisely because it is *God's* future and his
destiny for us.

God's sovereignty as we understand it here is not a matter of
a divine cause that brings forth a human effect, or theological de-
terminism. Because he is God, his sovereignty is expressed in the
exercise of our freedom when we move toward our self-actualiza-
tion as children of God. This means our freedom is taken seriously;
we are quite capable of defying the sovereignty of God. There is
nothing automatic about our relation to God for we are genuine
partners in that relationship. It may lead to great blessing and to
the realization, in Dante's words, that "In thy will is our peace."
On the other hand it may lead to bitter alienation and judgment.
In either case, the sovereignty of God is there in the destiny toward
which we are moving.

The God of Law

When we speak of God's judgment we think of his law, which
is another side of divine sovereignty. Our lives are renewed by the
Gospel, but a contrasting way in which we are addressed by God
is in what we might call the "law of life." This law is expressed in
Paul's observation in Galatians 6:7: "Do not be deceived; God is
not mocked, for whatever a man sows, that he will also reap." The

apostle expresses the same idea when he speaks of our accountability before God (Rom. 3:19). Our being held to account is the other side of our freedom; we cannot evade the one any more than we can deny the other. Our response to the demands that life places on us may be responsible or irresponsible, either enhancing our freedom or limiting it. If I refuse to meet my obligations to others, or exploit my relationships with others, I build a past which restricts my future and may even in many ways destroy it. The demands and opportunities of life are seen by the Christian as the means by which God speaks to us, calling us to account and therein calling us to ourselves because the ethical demands of life compel us to face the question of what it means to be human.

This view of law as the moral demands of life can be extended to include all those experiences which in one way or another coerce and limit us. These experiences do not deny the reality of our freedom but set the boundaries within which our freedom is challenged and expressed. The fact that we are born into a particular family, and at a particular time and place, may painfully restrict the possibilities open to us in the future. Or again, our talents and abilities have much to do with the opportunities available to us, a fact which may at times be quite difficult to accept. More frustrating yet can be the fortuitous happenings over which we have absolutely no control, and which close doors which we had thought would be open to us. Events and circumstances like these turn us back upon ourselves and challenge us to find the resources to respond. Once again, the Christian perceives in these life-experiences the encounter with God's law of life. Whenever we are forced to a moment of truth concerning ourselves and challenged to grow in coping with that moment, God is meeting us in a decisive way that has a bearing upon our future. It is in such moments that our lives are "on the line," and how we respond reveals ourselves both to others and to ourselves (though we may be unwilling to recognize what we see!).

We use the term "law," then, to describe the events and circumstances of life which challenge us to respond with integrity. Perhaps this is puzzling since law is not usually described in this way. We are used to thinking of law in terms of the Ten Commandments, or some code of moral behavior. But of course all such codes are the result of life-experiences in which we are challenged to act in a morally responsible way. Here we are concerned not with the content of the law but with the existential reality of one's *hearing* the law, or experiencing the demand of the law as it confronts us in the events and circumstances of our lives. People usually think of God as the law-giver, or even a kind of policeman who not only gives us the law but enforces it by keeping a steady eye on us. This understanding of God's sovereignty is not worthy of the Gospel. The presence of moral rules and laws is a testimony to our conscience and the efforts of society to maintain order. But as far as a Christian understanding of God and the law is concerned, the important thing is to recognize the call to integrity which law represents, and that we become more fully human by living lives that are morally responsible. This is where God is at. He does not enforce the law, he confronts us in it!

The God of Providence

It should be clear from our discussion both here and in other chapters that Christian faith affirms the presence of God in the events and circumstances of our lives, both in times of trial and judgment and in times of grace, liberation and renewal. Within the context of the doctrine of creation, this presence of God to his world has been called providence. In the classic understanding of creation as an event at the beginning of time, the doctrine of God's providence asserted that God had not left his world following creation but was actively involved in it. In the view of creation proposed in this chapter, in which creation is not a past event but a present reality to faith, providence becomes another term to express the conviction of faith that God is present to his creation in a purposeful way. We should note that belief in providence does *not* mean that nothing evil or unfortunate can happen to the believer. This notion is a crass illustration of what we have called idolatry in the guise of religion, where one's interest in God is simply to construct a measure of security for oneself.

Providence, rightly understood, includes God's judgment as well as his grace, for both are involved in the direction of a person's life. To experience God's demand and judgment is to turn away from evil, destructive paths. To experience his grace is to be renewed and strengthened in one's humanity and in constructive relationships with others. There is nothing mechanical or automatic about this sense of providence. There can be overpowering ambiguities and tragedies in one's life, but through it all the person of faith discerns a promise which is reflected in Paul's words, "We know that in everything God works for good with those who love him" (Rom. 8:28). The apostle's life, it might be recalled, was not exactly free of mental and physical suffering.

When we speak of providence in this way, the term is clearly a testimony to the faith of those who believe in providence, expressing their gratitude for blessings which may not be all that apparent to the disinterested observer. This faith is the basis for an affirmation of life and a joyful acceptance of the tasks we have been given to do. Providence should be contrasted to fate, where one resigns oneself in despair before the inevitable. The loss of the sense of providence today has turned people to a variety of means by which they seek to make themselves secure. Astrology is one notable example of this, providing a surprising number of people with the illusion that they can control the future. For people who believe in the providence of God, the concern is not to figure out what's going to happen next, but to live responsibly in a world entrusted to them as well as to recognize a God-given purpose and destiny to their lives.

The Christian understanding of providence is not based on an abstract notion of divine sovereignty and omnipotence. It does not mean that God is determining everything that happens. He is not subject to our ideas of his sovereignty and how it should be exercised in the world, for his sovereignty is his freedom and mystery. If we let the figure of Christ shape our idea of divine providence, then God exercises his sovereignty in servanthood and the healing and reconciling power of love. He becomes a part of our world and works within it, rather than operating by fiat outside of it. The God of creation for the Christian is the God of promise who encounters us in the biblical revelation. Consequently, the notion of providence points us ultimately to the destiny of our world where providence will find its consummation in a new order, prefigured in the resurrection of Jesus Christ.

The Problem of Evil

The greatest challenge to the Christian notion of God's sovereignty and his providential presence to the world is the searing reality of evil. We have already considered some aspects of this problem in our discussion of faith and human tragedy.[5] Here we must note some further dimensions of the problem in the context of divine providence. The logical problem posed for Christians (or anyone who believes in a God of providence) is this: If God is truly sovereign, and if God is love, then why are the powers of evil so prevalent in human history? One is forced to the conclusion that either God is sovereign but not a God of love, or God is love but not sovereign. Apparently we must speak either of a God of love whose power is limited or an omnipotent God whose power is something else than love. However, this dilemma clearly assumes a model of God's relation to the world in which God is the "divine determiner" who is responsible for all that happens, a view we have already rejected. One can go on to argue that such a view would also be a denial of human freedom, and as long as there is human freedom there must be the possibility of evil. But then one asks, "Is not the evil in the world too great a price for our freedom?" Or again, "Could not God have created a creature with freedom but without the capacity for such devastating acts of evil?"

These kinds of arguments are too abstract and hypothetical, failing to get at the existential seriousness of the problem of evil. Those who agonize over it and convey its impact most compellingly are those who have been outraged by the suffering of the innocent, particularly the suffering of children. We noted this protest in the work of Camus; Dostoevsky reflects the same sense of horror in a famous passage from *The Brothers Karamazov* (Book V, Chapter 4). Ivan is speaking:

> It's not worth the tears of that one tortured child who beat himself on the breast with its little fist and prayed in its stinking

outhouse with an unexpiated tear to "dear, kind God"! It's not worth it, because those tears are unatoned for. They must be atoned for, or there can be no harmony. But how? How are you going to atone for them? Is it possible? By their being avenged? But what do I care for avenging them? What do I care for a hell for oppressors? What good can hell do, since those children have already been tortured? And what becomes of harmony, if there is hell? I want to forgive. I want to embrace. I don't want more suffering. And if the suffering of children go to swell the sum of suffering which was necessary to pay for truth, then I protest that the truth is not worth such a price.

It is small consolation to answer the Ivans of the world by saying that evil is a necessary aspect of a world in which there are free beings, even if it is true. The distinctively Christian answer to the problem of evil is to be found in the very nature of the Gospel. If we define God's sovereignty in light of the revelation in Christ, it is a sovereignty of love whose purposes will be realized in the future. But the God of love has entered into the suffering of our world and has shared that suffering with us. The painful reality of innocent suffering is symbolized in the cross, for the crucifixion was a brutal assault on an innocent victim. One dimension of the good news which emerges from that event is that suffering that appears pointless and destructive can become redemptive. To believe in the sovereignty of God who is love is to affirm the transforming power of that love which is able to make all things new. The reality of that love is not always apparent in the world, but its presence provides us with grounds for hope as we look to the future.

The Christian conviction that God is involved in the travail of human history has obvious implications for those who claim that conviction. As far as their own suffering is concerned, they are comforted in knowing that they are not alone, that there is one who has gone before them who also suffered and overcame. In regard to the evil they encounter in the world, the exploitation of the weak and the suffering of the innocent, Christians know that the only appropriate answer is to become involved in overcoming it. Because Christian faith points us to the future and the fulfillment of human life which is promised by the Gospel of the resurrection, the Christian cannot lose heart but lives with an abiding trust in that promise.

God in Current Theology

In view of the extensive criticism of traditional theism, it is not surprising that a number of new and creative ways of thinking about God have emerged in recent years. In this concluding section we shall briefly describe two of these approaches which have become particularly significant for American theology. Both of them involve a reorientation in the metaphysical picture of God and his relation to the world. It is contended that this reorientation is necessary both in order to capture the biblical view of God and to carry out the theological task more effectively in our times. These two new directions are process theology and the theology of hope.

Process Theology

In our discussion of the task of theology (Chapter 2), we noted that theologians never operate in a vacuum, but in a particular cultural situation to which they address the Gospel message. This activity is a two-way street, in which theologians reflect the thinking and attitudes of their era at the same time as they interpret the Gospel to their culture. Today, the way in which we understand and interpret the universe and our place within it has been profoundly influenced by the scientific revolutions of the nineteenth and twentieth centuries. If one were to select a single concept to capture the view of the world engendered by science, it could well be the word, "process." Both in biology through Darwin and in physics through Einstein, time has become an important dimension to reality, which we see no longer as static and fixed but in a state of process or evolution.

Two figures from the scientific world have exerted great influence on many theologians by bringing the concepts of process and evolution into the realm of theology. They are the mathematician,

Alfred North Whitehead (1861-1947), and the Jesuit paleontologist to whom we have referred several times, Teilhard de Chardin. The philosophy of Whitehead, who spent his later years developing a metaphysics based on the notion of process, has engendered a rather well-defined theological school which goes by the name of "process theology." Our discussion will focus on the theology of those influenced by Whitehead, represented by such theologians as Bernard Meland, Daniel Day Williams, Norman Pittenger, John B. Cobb, Jr., and Schubert Ogden.

Process theologians have been primarily concerned with the doctrine of God. They have vigorously criticized the classical view coming from Aristotle and Aquinas, in which God is pure being over against a world of becoming. They regard this view as dualistic in separating God from the world, for the God who is all-sufficient and impassible (not affected by change) can hardly be involved with us in genuine relationship. The world may be dependent upon him, but he can in no way be dependent on the world. Rather than the traditional theism, process theologians propose a view which is characterized by the word *panentheism,* in which God is both in and distinct from (though not apart from) the cosmic process. Where theism speaks of transcendence and immanence, process theologians reject a transcendence which places the reality of God apart from the cosmos. God must be integrally related to the world so that his very being is defined in terms of his relationship to it.

In accomplishing this objective, process theologians espouse a "dipolar" view of God which is found in Whitehead's philosophy. God has both a primordial nature in which he is the ground of all activity, and a consequent nature in which the world reacts upon God. God's primordial nature is not defined over against the world, however, but is realized in the concrete actualizations occurring within the world. This is his consequent nature in which God is interacting in the cosmos and receiving into himself the occurrences of the world, thereby becoming the occasion for new and better realizations or concretions in the ongoing process. God is thus a part of the whole process of becoming which characterizes the world. Whitehead rejects the notion of a "creation out of nothing," maintaining instead that creation is a continuous process in which God has no temporal priority. God "is not *before* all creation but *with* all creation."

The language of the preceding paragraph concerning God's relation to the world, including such words as "occurrences" and "concretions," is likely puzzling to most readers. This language reflects the metaphysics of Whitehead, who asks that we get beyond the commonsense perception of the world in which we are subjects in a world of objects, or things. The basic category is not things but events, or energy-events. Whitehead speaks of "actual entities" as the units or "building blocks" of the universe, meaning not things but events. It is the kind of language which physicists might use to describe the world. Process theologians go on (following Whitehead) to use the category of event to conceive of God. God is a dynamic event who is the "eminent" or "exemplary" case of this basic metaphysical principle in the cosmos. This dynamic view of God and the cosmos includes a universal movement or direction toward a self-fulfilling goal involving God in relation to everything else. He is both cause and recipient of all that happens in the world.

With this involvement in the events of the world, the God of process theology reflects the biblical faith that God is affected by the hurts and aspirations of human life. The very reality of God is tied up with the quest for meaning and fulfillment which motivates the life of individual and society. The problem of evil is also answered more effectively, say the process theologians. God is not the omnipotent, sovereign law-giver and judge who "allows" evil to flourish. God's power is the persuasion of love, appropriate to the freedom of human beings. The very presence of values and structures of goodness and meaning in which God is involved also makes possible the evils of corruption. Thus God is responsible for evil only in the sense that evil is the corruption of the good which God is bringing into being. Without the capacity for love there would be no sin as the failure to love.

Process theology has a problem of communication because of its esoteric metaphysical concepts. Though it is addressing our historical experience when it speaks of process, its language is nonetheless highly abstract. Its concepts appear to its critics to be but tenuously related to the world of experience which they would systematize and explain, and some argue that this kind of metaphysics is as difficult to pursue in our time as the traditional theological language which it attacks. The point is also argued that process theology lacks the autonomy over its philosophical roots which is necessary for any responsible theology. Whitehead's philosophy exercises too decisive an influence.

Theology of Hope

The theology of hope, also called theology of promise or futurist theology, replaces the vertical line which usually characterizes Christian thinking about God with a horizontal line. Instead of picturing God above us and present to us in mystery, the theology of hope directs us to the future in order to find God. It replaces a spatial metaphor with a temporal one in which God is before us as "the power of the future." In presenting this view of God, theologians of hope would recapture the eschatological character of the biblical message. This means that they are intent on shaping Christian theology according to the end or consummation towards which the human story is moving. The God of the Bible is not fully known in the present but is known as *promise,* turning us to the future in anticipation and hope. We are pilgrims, we are on the way, and the fulfillment of life is never completely present but beckons us from the future. To believe in the God of scripture is to affirm our destiny in God who is always before us, and who enables us to live in the hope inspired by his promise.

A fundamental idea to the theology of hope is the ontological priority of the future, an idea found in the writings of the German Marxist philosopher, Ernst Bloch. Wolfhart Pannenberg, one of the principal theologians of hope, has developed this idea as a basis for his theology. He maintains that futurity is not simply a characteristic of our existence, it is the most appropriate notion for God himself. God is not a timeless being but the ultimate future whose power draws the human story to its consummation. We usually think of the nature of something as determined by its origin, but Pannenberg maintains that what something is is determined by its destiny. We are who we shall be, a point that was noted in our discussion of human nature (Chapter 3). As our ultimate future, God is before us, encouraging us in our freedom to choose the way to our own self-realization and fulfillment.

One of the fascinating aspects of the theology of hope is its fruitful contact with Marxist thought. It is often observed that Karl Marx's vision of the classless society reflects Christian eschatology, in which the kingdom of God is secularized and made a goal which is realizable through an economic reordering of society. The goal-oriented character of our lives has been powerfully elaborated by Ernst Bloch. He sees the human being as fundamentally one who hopes and dreams until the possible is turned into reality. He maintains that Jesus' message was revolutionary in directing his contemporaries to a utopian future he called the kingdom of God. Subsequently this horizontal direction of Jesus' teaching was changed into a vertical concept, heaven, and the result was to drain the revolutionary power from Jesus' message. Theologians of hope like the Protestant, Jürgen Moltmann, and the Roman Catholic, Johannes Metz, reflect the influence of these ideas. They stress the revolutionary social implications of the church's message, for when it is rightly understood it is a message which challenges the status quo in the name of the God who calls us to be open to the future.

The theology of hope has made a significant contribution to current Christian thinking about God. Its strength and appeal is based first on its recapturing the eschatological, future-directed character of biblical thought and Christian experience. In addition it speaks effectively to the contemporary mind when it "locates" God in the future. In an age which speaks of the loss of transcendence, the theology of hope answers quite rightly that according to Christian faith we never possess God in his fullness, but live on the basis of the promise which is inherent in the life, death and resurrection of Jesus Christ. To live by faith is to live by hope.

The question can be raised, however, whether it is necessary to make such exclusive alternatives of the horizontal and vertical modes of discourse concerning God. Actually both modes have lived together with each other and are likely dependent on each other. To emphasize the future, the tendency is to contrast future with present. The result is that God appears to have forsaken the present, or he is not yet present, or he is present only as promise. But if there is no presence of God which is more than promise, can there be any promise for the future? Without maintaining some kind of doctrine of divine providence as present reality, can one speak of God whose sovereignty is to be fully realized in the future? Or one might ask whether the secular person finds any more credible the notion of God who comes to us as the power of the future than in such present realities as judgment and grace. There also remains a significant leap between that understanding of the future which sees its promise as dependent upon the course taken by an enlightened humankind, and that view of faith which sees the future as the coming of God in fulfillment of his promise. But in spite of these observations it is certainly true that the horizontal way of thinking bears a particularly effective message for our own times.

Though using different concepts, both process theology and the theology of hope are future-oriented, historical and immanental in character. The former is much more bound to a particular philosophy with its distinctive language, while the latter, though influenced by certain philosophical viewpoints, uses a language which has been more immediately shaped by theologians. This in itself is reason for the greater influence of the theology of hope today.

Our own discussion of God and the human situation certainly betrays the influence of futurist thinking. At the same time we have stressed the existential moment, or the *kairos* (fullness of time) of the present in one's coming to faith and consciously entering into the presence of God. The reality of death, which any existential viewpoint faces quite squarely, has run throughout our discussion and has raised in its most intense form the question of our future. As mortal creatures, death is the final reality of life. Here is where the existential and eschatological meet in the Christian proclamation, in the form of death and resurrection. The resurrection of Jesus Christ conveys the message of hope that the future truly does belong to God.

8

Faith
Active in Community

IN THIS CHAPTER WE WANT TO STRESS a very important point concerning Christian faith: it brings people together in community. We have noted that faith is very much an individual matter, a venture and a risk that must be taken by the individual for himself, for no one else can take it for him. Yet the commitment to Jesus Christ by its very nature results in community, for it is a commitment that begs to be shared, celebrated, and put to work together with others. This community of faith we call the church, and as an institution with a long history it often creates ambivalent feelings even (or especially!) among Christians. Because it poses such an obstacle to many people, we must examine carefully just what Christians believe concerning the church. We begin by considering the work of the Spirit of God, which Christians relate specifically to the community of faith; then we attempt to get at the nature of the church by considering the ambiguities involved in some basic affirmations about the church, and close with a discussion of the vital center of the church's life, its worship and the relation of worship to mission.

The Holy Spirit and the Community of Faith

When Christians begin to talk about the Spirit, their listeners will often become uneasy. The word itself is difficult to nail down; its meaning is quite nebulous for many people. Moreover, serious talk about the Spirit conveys something quite personal about our own life. It may relate to a moving experience which is meaningful to us because of our faith in God, and our listeners may have no

152

idea what we are talking about. Christians speak of the Spirit when they want to say something about the *presence* of God in their lives or in the human story as a whole. In other words, the Spirit expresses God *at work* in our lives, both as agent and as power. To speak of God as Holy Spirit is to express the mystery, the presence and the power of God—enough to make anyone uneasy!

But the question arises: How do you know if the power or the presence you experience is the Holy Spirit and not some other source or dimension of human experience? Christians have to acknowledge the ambiguity of every reference to the Spirit, recognizing also the many ways in which the term is misused. But there is a context of common experience and tradition provided by the community of faith which helps Christians to be responsible in their reference to the Spirit of God. It is the Gospel of Jesus Christ which has introduced them to the Spirit in their own lives, and therefore that Gospel becomes the criterion for their reference to the Spirit. The apostle Paul even interchanges the Spirit of God with the Spirit of Jesus as the one exalted by God through the resurrection. This does not mean that the Spirit of God is at work in the Christian witness alone, but that witness becomes for Christians the basis on which they understand the presence of God in the world, or God the Spirit.

The church, or the community of faith, is essential to any discussion of the Holy Spirit. In the third article of the Apostles' Creed, Christians confess, "I believe in the Holy Spirit, the holy catholic [1] church, the communion of saints. . . ." These words express the conviction of Christians that they have been drawn together by the presence of God in their world. That presence creates community, expressing the truth that we are not created for ourselves alone, but for each other. The work of the Spirit points us to the destiny of human life, and the church, with all its imperfections, seeks to express that destiny in its life of witness and service.

The book of the Acts of the Apostles in the New Testament has been quite important to the church's understanding of itself as a creation of the Holy Spirit. The second chapter tells the story of what happened at the Jewish festival of Pentecost following the resurrection of Jesus. It describes the outpouring of the Spirit, an event marked by unusual happenings. There was a sound from heaven "like the rush of a mighty wind" that filled the house where people had gathered; there appeared "tongues as of fire" resting on each of them; there was speaking in tongues which foreigners who had gathered in Jerusalem recognized as their own language; the experience led some to accuse the Christians of being drunk; and Peter, the disciple of Jesus, delivered such a powerful message that "about three thousand souls" accepted the Gospel of Jesus Christ.

The story of Pentecost makes use of unusual phenomena—rushing wind, tongues of fire, speaking in a language other than one's own—to symbolize the meaning of the new experience of faith in the resurrected Jesus. Biblical scholarship has helped us to recognize a highly stylized piece of work in this story, involving considerable theological reflection on the part of the author, Luke. The Jewish festival of Pentecost was the appropriate time for the outpouring of the Spirit because it was the anniversary of Moses' giving of the law on Mount Sinai. In this way the new covenant in Christ is related to the old covenant given by Moses. Jesus is the new Moses to whom the Old Testament points. The rushing of wind symbolizes the coming of the Spirit. Speaking in tongues conveys the utter transcendence of the Spirit who is incapable of being grasped by our speech and yet who reaches beyond our human divisions to communicate the mighty works of God. Thus Pentecost stands as the answer of God to the story of Babel (Gen. 11:1-9), where as a result of its pride the human race was judged and confounded by losing its common language and the power of communication. The Spirit recreates the human community as it was intended, a point that Luke stresses again in his inclusion of the Gentiles (Acts 10) as well as the Jews in the experience of the Spirit. The Spirit embraces the whole human race.

A literal understanding of the Pentecost story together with statements of Paul concerning "gifts of the spirit" have led many in the church to identify the Holy Spirit with unusual or miraculous acts. Paul mentions in 1 Corinthians 12-14 such gifts as speaking in tongues, healing, and performing wondrous works. Here the Spirit is treated as a power which expresses itself in moments of ecstasy or in unusual gifts. We know that worship in Corinth was characterized by ecstatic experiences in which people spoke in tongues, but Paul argues that anything that is incomprehensible is inferior to what is truly edifying, such as the gift of prophecy (which is not forecasting the future but revealing the truth that is hidden to us [1 Cor. 14:25]). He acknowledges other "works of the Spirit" according to his criteria of what contributes toward building up the community of faith, such as service to others *(diakonia)*. The conclusion we get from Paul is that we ought not exalt those ecstatic experiences that can occur in religious life, but let the Spirit express his presence in a life of service and love (1 Cor. 13).

But in spite of Paul's critique of the ecstatic gifts, he does not deny them as expressions of the Spirit if through them Christ is confessed and the faith-community is built up. These gifts can be seen as one particular expression within the variety of Christian experience, but they are not particularly important to the church as a whole. The danger is that Christians identify God's presence with unusual happenings, reflecting the all-too-human tendency to associate the Spirit with any kind of intensely-felt or even bizarre event. Periodically through the centuries the church has experienced times of revival or awakening in which unusual events occurred, but such periods should not provide us with a stereotyped understanding of what it means to be filled with the Spirit. Wherever there is the experience of grace in the midst of human failure; wherever the Gospel is joyfully and thankfully appropriated in faith; wherever lives are transformed or renewed through encounter with the Gospel—there we testify to the presence of God the Holy Spirit among us. In light of the criterion of the Gospel, such questions as these are appropriate in evaluating claims to be filled with the Spirit: Is Christ glorified? Is the Gospel exercising its healing power? Is the church of Christ strengthened? When these things are happening the Christian community gives thanks for realities which it has no power to dispense or control. It is testimony to the presence of God the Holy Spirit among his people.

When we bring Holy Spirit and church together and regard the church as an article of faith, it is important to note that we are not identifying the church with God so that it becomes in any way a divine institution. Any Christian with a reasonable degree of honesty can testify to the all-too-human character of the church. But Christian faith affirms that while the church is obviously a sociological entity with all the imperfections of any group of people who congregate together, it is also a theological entity. It is a community that understands its mission and destiny in light of Jesus Christ, and consequently what the church really is depends on who Jesus really is. Faith in the triune God thus carries with it a faith in the church as one manifestation of the work of the triune God, but this faith turns us to the future for its ultimate vindication. In looking at the church as a present reality, the Christian must readily acknowledge the tension between the ideal and the real, the church as it is called to be and the church as it really is. This is a tension which permeates every discussion of the church.

Is the Church for Real?

Theologians have often written about the church in language which many people think is far removed from reality. It is theological language which expresses Christian convictions, but it always raises the painful question whether the *real* church is not something else from what is being described. Take, for example, the New Testament letter to the Ephesians, where Paul speaks of the church as the "body" of Christ (1:23), united with Christ as "members of his body." He describes the church as "a holy temple in the Lord" (2:21), a people who are "cleansed" that they "might be holy and without blemish" (5:27). Theologians have gone on to speak of the church as a redemptive community, and some have gone so far as to say it is the extension of the incarnation itself, embodying the saving work of Christ in the world.

Obviously this is the language of faith, but how is it to be reconciled with the less-than-inspiring realities of church history? One looks at the medieval church and is impressed with the arrogance of power, the exploitation of the pious masses, and the self-centered ambition of many of its leaders. Look at the members of any Christian congregation today and you are likely to find the moral vices which are common to our society as a whole. How is this fact to be reconciled with the demands of Christian discipleship? This kind of discrepancy is what the non-Christian is most likely to notice, but there are other problems as well. For example, in view of the church's claim to be the "body of Christ," why is it so hopelessly divided? Why is one church so hostile towards another if their members are brothers and sisters "in Christ"? Christians have even gone to war against each other in the name of Christ!

Perhaps the best way to examine these problems as well as to get at the nature of the church as such, is to consider the ancient confession which states that the church is "one, holy, catholic, and apostolic." The tensions between the real church and what the church is called to be are clearly apparent in each of these adjectives.

The Divided Church

To say that the church is "one" or united is obviously not true in regard to the empirical organization of the church. In the United States alone there are close to three hundred different churches (though many are very small, consisting of a few congregations). In order to understand if not appreciate this proliferation of Christian communions, one must be acquainted with the history of the church in this country. The nature of Protestantism, which has stressed the individual's direct access to God rather than through an ecclesiastical institution, plus the desire of our founding fathers to avoid the establishment of a state church, has resulted in an atmosphere which has encouraged the emergence of many churches. We call them "denominations," meaning that it is a "free church" situation in which no church enjoys a privileged status in relation to the state. Many Christians argue that the existence of these denominations is not an evil in itself, for they testify to the variety of Christian experience and allow like-minded Christians to find a fellowship and a spiritual atmosphere in which they feel at home.

On the other hand, the denominational picture presents a fragmented church. Some denominations were started as a result of personality clashes between church leaders, in which the offended party has picked up his marbles and led his followers into a new church of his own making. Intense theological controversies have also led to divisions, as in the fundamentalist-modernist conflict during the early decades of this century. Tensions over the slavery issue led to the formation of new denominations in the South. Both theological and non-theological factors have been at work in the forming of new churches, but whatever the reasons, the end result has tended to trivialize the church in the eyes of the world. Where is the unity of the church in view of these divisions?

Protestant theology maintains that the unity of the church is not to be found in its organization. In fact, nothing achieved by the church could constitute its unity. The only source of unity is Jesus Christ himself. The unity in Christ transcends the divisions of the church, no matter how divided they may be as a result of human weakness. At the same time, it is the task of the church to express its unity in Christ in every way possible, for it is more than likely that division will compromise the effectiveness of the church's witness to Christ. But theologians disagree over whether complete organizational unity is desirable. It is of course true that divisions within the church that reflect suspicion and animosity toward fellow-Christians are to be condemned as an expression of the most insidious kind of sin, religious pride. But the variety of Christian experience and consequent differences in forms of worship and theological interpretations of the Gospel will understandably result in a variety of Christian churches, particularly where a free church situation prevails.

Roman Catholicism has a different answer to the problem of unity. It maintains that the church from the beginning has had an authoritative office, instituted by Jesus himself when he designated his disciple, Peter, as the "rock" upon which his church would be built (Matt. 16:13ff.). This office is identified with the papacy, and the Pope, as the "vicar of Christ," is the proper head of the church. The unity of the church is consequently identified with the papal office, which means that Roman Catholicism has, in contrast to Protestantism, a tangible principle of unity. If you are in communion with the church of Rome, you are part of the church. Jesus Christ is indeed the cornerstone of the church (Eph. 2:20), but the church's unity is determined by the Petrine office which he instituted.

The painful reality of church disunity has been a principal con-

cern of twentieth-century Christians. Undoubtedly the most significant development in the church during this century has been the
ecumenical movement, which is the attempt of churches throughout
the world to give tangible expression to their unity. The World
Council of Churches, which embodies both Protestant and Eastern
Orthodox churches, is the principal organization spearheading this
movement on an international scale. It did not include the Roman
Catholic Church to any appreciable degree until Pope John XXIII
"opened the windows" of his church by convening the Second
Vatican Council in 1962. As a result of that Council, a new spirit
of openness was unleashed among Catholics toward the Eastern
and Protestant churches. Non-Catholic Christians were hailed as
separated brethren, and theological conversations have since been
initiated between Catholic theologians and representatives of a
variety of Christian traditions. Discussions and cooperative ventures
have multiplied among Catholics and Protestants on every level of
church life. But of course the divisions of centuries cannot be removed in a few years or even a few decades. The institutional character of churches results in built-in efforts to preserve themselves.
The officials of any church as well as the vast majority of its membership are inclined to defend the institutional status quo because
they have developed institutional loyalties (for the officials it's also
their jobs!) whose roots are deep. To take ecumenism seriously
demands openness to the possibility of one's own church being
merged with others, and though this has been happening regularly
in the past few decades, it is never easy. It demands from church
leadership both a compelling vision of the church's unity as well as
a sense of urgency about realizing that unity, otherwise the institutional loyalties already present will continue to prevail.

Few people can imagine a time when the church's unity will be
expressed in the form of one organized church. Even if most Christians were someday to belong to one church, there would inevitably
be splinter-churches resulting from disagreements of various kinds.
Since the sixteenth century Protestant Reformation there have been
two major church traditions in the West, Roman Catholicism and
Protestantism. These two traditions, together with the Orthodox
churches in the East, constitute the three major communions of

Christianity. Historically, Roman Catholicism has maintained that the union of Christendom would have to involve a return of the other two traditions to the Roman Catholic fold under the supremacy of the Pope. The expression of this attitude has softened since Vatican II, and yet it is obvious, given the strong hierarchical structure of Catholicism, that any future church would include the papal office in some form.

Some Protestant theologians have suggested that the papacy could serve as the visible symbol of the universal church in the future if it were thoroughly reformed. It could become primarily a pastoral rather than a juridical office, with the decisions of church leadership made in a more democratic fashion involving significant representation of the people, or laity. Since Vatican II there has been continuous agitation for democratization within Roman Catholicism, the results of which are becoming increasingly visible. These developments are quite significant for the future of the ecumenical movement, for they have set in motion forces of convergence which establish more common ground between Catholics and Protestants. Although there has been much disillusionment with ecumenism since the euphoria of the 1960s occasioned by Pope John XXIII, there remains good reason for optimism if one takes a longer, historical view. The important thing for Christians to recognize today is that it is irresponsible to be anything but an ecumenical Christian.

Should the church ever accomplish organizational unity, it would clearly have to allow considerable freedom within its structures for a variety of forms of worship and expressions of the Christian life. If true to the Gospel of Christ, such a church would maintain unity without an insistence on uniformity. There are churches that are strongly ethnic in character, churches with fairly rigid, authoritarian structures, and churches which stress individual freedom and look with suspicion on organizational forms beyond the level of the local congregation. There are churches which practice a rigorous, puritanical morality and churches whose members could hardly survive one day under that morality. But even without organizational unity, the goals of the ecumenical vision would be reached to a significant degree if all churches arrived at the point where each could appreciate the distinctive contribution made by the others to the total expression of the Christian church. There is need of understanding the historical background of each church so that its unique character and gifts can be recognized. If the fundamental unity of the church is recognized in the common confession of faith in the triune God and the lordship of Jesus Christ, then we are free to appreciate what each church has to contribute within that unity to the overwhelming richness and variety of Christian experience.

The Hypocritical Church

The Christian confesses that the church is "holy," an offensive assertion to many who stand outside of the church and observe the less than holy character of many of its members. But the word as it is used here needs some explanation if one is to rightly understand its meaning. It does not mean that those in the church are morally perfect or even a shade better than those outside of the church. Just as the unity of the church is given in Christ, so the holiness of the church is no achievement of Christians but the gift of God. To be holy in a scriptural sense is to be called out to a holy purpose, to carry out the mission of God who is holy. The New Testament word used to denote the church, *ekklesia* (from which comes the word, "ecclesiastical"), conveys this idea of being "called out." It is the calling of God that makes holiness a reality for the church. This also accounts for Paul's use of the word "saints" to describe believers, as well as the confession of faith in the church as "the communion of saints."

But just as the gift of unity in Christ constitutes a task for the church to realize, so the holiness of the church constitutes a task. A holy people should be an instrument in God's hands to carry out his purposes. Here there is disagreement between Protestants and Roman Catholics in understanding the expression of holiness in the church. Protestants stress the forgiveness of sins bestowed by God through the Word and sacraments. The holy person is the forgiven person. Catholics also understand holiness in terms of a gift of God, but that gift is seen as sacramental grace which forms a habit or character to the believer which makes one acceptable to

God. To the Protestant this appears as a dilution of God's sovereign grace in the creation of a holy people, making the gift a cooperative project between the believer and God rather than a pure gift of God. Catholics respond by saying that they are taking seriously the need of an appropriate human response to God's grace, a point which they believe is too easily lost in the Protestant emphasis upon "grace alone."

The hypocrisy of the church lies in its lukewarm response to the mission of Jesus Christ in the world. It is not true to its calling because of a lack of faith in its leader—which means a failure to follow its leader. The Sermon on the Mount (Matt. 5-7) challenges the followers of Jesus to a life of radical love which generally appears to have been ignored by church members. It is not a calling to be good and moral like other upright people in society, but a more radical calling to be "the salt of the earth," the "leaven" in the world. This kind of life involves going the second mile and taking risks beyond what duty would require. Can the church really fulfill this mission?

Christians disagree over what needs to be done in the church to enable it to respond positively to this question. The major churches in this country—what are often called the mainline denominations —are for the most part inclusive churches. This means that there are no requirements for membership other than a profession of faith (usually after a period of instruction) and the stated intention to be faithful in worship and in living the life of Christian discipleship. But the implications of membership are rarely explored in any systematic fashion by church members. Because of its institutional character and its image in our society, the church is more likely joined for a sense of neighborhood belonging, for business reasons, or family pressures. A look at any typical congregation will reveal substantial differences among its members in their understanding of Christian faith and its implications for their attitudes and actions in society. It is usually a rather small core of members who possess a well-informed sense of Christian responsibility and who are seriously concerned about the meaning and implications of their faith.

Those who disagree with the inclusiveness of most churches maintain that the church must be exclusive in its membership policy if it is to be a genuine and effective Christian community. Various standards have been used in order to insure this. Some churches have insisted that each member be able to testify to a religious conversion at a particular time and place. These churches want only "born again" Christians, for without an indelible conversion experience they doubt the genuineness of one's faith. Others have advocated the withdrawal of serious-minded Christians into house churches in order to experience a more genuine fellowship. During the 1960s there were many cell groups of Christians who were disillusioned with the lack of social consciousness on the part of the institutional church and who pronounced judgment upon it by withdrawing in small groups of like-minded Christians. Here a sense of social responsibility was the implicit criterion for Christian fellowship. In view of the major domestic problem of racism, some have advocated excommunicating those persons who are clearly guilty of racist activity. Until some years ago the Methodist Church required its membership to refrain from drinking alcoholic beverages because the evils of excessive drinking were destructive of family and social values.

One may commend the seriousness of purpose in these attempts to overcome hypocrisy in the church, but they are no solution. Not only is there the difficulty of deciding what standard should be applied; there is also the problem of how to maintain the purity of the fellowship in light of that standard. If a community of Christians wants to apply a standard for membership that is in any way enforceable, it will be too narrow a standard to capture the whole range of Christian faith and responsibility. It would be a standard that picks out and absolutizes one particular dimension of faith or practice. If it seeks to enforce that standard it runs the risk of legalism, which is contrary to the spirit of the church's message. Because that message is God's acceptance of the sinner, the church can hardly place restrictions on those who want to hear it and share in the fellowship created by that message. The church must remain inclusive, despite the problems and frustrations that are involved. The only answer appears to be the slow and difficult task of preaching and teaching and counseling the Gospel of Jesus Christ so that it confronts people in their particular situation. One cannot create an appropriate response to the Gospel by setting up rules or exercising judgment. People must be persuaded by the Gospel itself.

There have been many harsh judgments pronounced on the church in recent times. Not only is its hypocrisy scored, but also the irrelevance and triviality of much of its activity. One painful characteristic of church life today is its reflection of the values of the consumer culture in which we live. Madison Avenue techniques are eagerly aped in "selling" the Gospel. Church services become productions, pastors become performers, and church activities become "fun events" which compete with other neighborhood attractions. One church featured parachutists landing in its parking lot as a gimmick to increase attendance; another featured Ronald McDonald handing out 5,000 fishburgers as a twentieth century version of Jesus feeding the 5,000 with loaves and fishes. Even among church leaders there is often a lack of sensitivity to the tension between the church's message and the self-indulgent character of a consumer society.

The frequent failure of the church to challenge injustice in our society has been another cause for the charge of hypocrisy. The institutional character of the church, with its ties to the establishment, often prevent it from exercising its prophetic function. The prophets spoke out against the rich and the powerful for what they were doing to the poor and the powerless. But the church finds the rich and the powerful in its pews on Sunday morning, with the result that pastors and bishops are not as inclined to act the role of the prophet. At the same time one must also recognize that in general the church today has become more sensitive to its social responsibility. In many ways the church has become an advocate for those who suffer from oppressive social structures, as well as continuing and expanding its traditional areas of work among the sick and afflicted.

Dwight L. Moody, the nineteenth century evangelist, was once stopped by a gentleman who complained at some length about the hypocrites he found in the church. Moody replied, "Why don't you join the church? There's always room for one more." Hypocrisy is a universal phenomenon that is no respecter of persons. In bearing the name of Christ, Christians of course are particularly vulnerable to the charge in view of the radical demand that Jesus places upon his followers. But for the church as a whole as well as for the individual Christian, the final answer to the gap between what it is called to be and what it really is is to be found in the grace of God. The church also lives by grace; it is also *simul iustus et peccator* (justified and a sinner at the same time). It can claim no perfection for itself, but can claim the forgiving grace of God and in that grace it can live. Such grace provides the promise and the confidence for the church as it seeks to carry out its mission.

The Closed Church

Christians confess their faith in the catholic or universal church, and once again we are confronted with what appears to be a contradiction. Where is the universal church? If the term means that the church embraces all people, then it is clearly not universal. In this sense of universality, the Roman Catholic Church comes closest to attaining it in virtue of its size and extensive geographical reach. Yet its universality is clearly compromised by the presence of other churches. Many Protestant churches, on the other hand, appear highly sectarian and make no pretense to universality.

But the church's universality is something else than this. It is catholic in the sense that it reaches out to all people. Its mission compels it to be all-embracing, for the Gospel of Jesus Christ is no respecter of persons. Paul's assertion in his letter to the Galatians is a beautiful expression of this fact:

> For as many of you as were baptized into Christ have put on Christ. There is neither Jew nor Greek, there is neither slave nor free, there is neither male nor female; for you are all one in Christ Jesus (Gal. 3:27-28).

In its expression of this universality the Christian sees the church as the symbol of God's purpose for his creation. It points us to the kingdom of God as the culmination and goal of the historical process and of all creation.

Once again we recognize the tension between what the church is to be and what it really is. Its openness to the world and all-embracing character are too often compromised by the divisions which mark our society. Divisions of social class, race, and ethnic heritage make their way into the church and prevent it from being a totally open community. Indeed, sociologists tell us that the Christian congregation will usually reflect to an exaggerated degree those divisions which are found in its social environment. The fellowship of the church easily becomes a chumminess among insiders, while the mission to reach out to the surrounding community is seen as a threat rather than an opportunity. The result is that the church appears to be more of a closed than an open fellowship.

At the same time we must recognize the considerable moral force which is inherent in the Christian conviction that we are all sons and daughters of the living God, whose good news would reconcile and unite the human family. It takes this kind of religious conviction for people to steadfastly and fearlessly struggle to overcome the divisive wounds in our society, regardless of cost. The church is in fact the seedbed from which has grown many an awakened conscience. Given its inclusive character, we cannot expect the church as a whole to be a task force in directly assaulting the divisions of society, but we can expect and in many instances do find in the church the resources for effecting reconciliation. At its best, the church recognizes and seeks to realize its own calling to be open to the world, creating a fellowship that would embrace all people.

The mission of the church to be open to the world has led some theologians to blur the identity of the church as a community of faith and a distinctive entity within the world. Some would have the church encompass all those whose lives reveal an openness to God, whatever their religious belief. One prominent reason for this view is that from ancient times the church has asserted that "outside of the church there is no salvation" (*extra ecclesiam nulla salus*). Since salvation is commonly understood as one's eternal destiny, it appears that the church is consigning most people to hell! In order to avoid this, theologians have expanded the boundaries of the church to embrace an invisible fellowship going well beyond the limits of church membership. But then the church becomes meaningless because it has no boundaries, no identity. A better solution is to limit the church to the historical community which professes faith in the risen Lord, and get rid of the notion that the church is for those who are "going to heaven." The pretensions that are inherent to such a claim are actually destructive of the kind of community that the church is called to be. While the Gospel does point us to a destiny beyond the grave, the church usurps the sovereignty of God whenever it claims to control that destiny.

Defining the Authentic Church

When we speak of the apostolicity of the church, we mean that the church is authentic when it is faithful to the witness of the apostles. The apostles are eyewitnesses of the events they report, and their proclamation (kerygma) has a fundamental and normative importance for all the preaching and teaching that follows. Very early in the history of the church, it was necessary to combat false witnesses and the emergence of heretical groups. The authentic community was compelled to demonstrate the continuity of its own witness with that of the apostles in order to show that they were the faithful community. For that reason, Christians defined the church in terms of its faithfulness to the apostolic witness concerning Jesus Christ.

There are significant differences between Roman Catholicism and Protestantism in their understanding of what constitutes the church's apostolicity. For Catholicism, the office of bishop, or the episcopate (the Greek word for bishop is *episkopas*) is fundamental to the authentic church. Early in the church's history that office became quite strategic as the source of authoritative teaching, thereby establishing the continuity of the church with the apostles. This identification of the episcopal office with the church's authenticity led to the view that bishops are the successors of the apostles and are indispensable to the church's identity. "Where the bishop is there is the church." With the bishop in Rome assuming a dominant position in the church's life, the papacy emerged as that office which defined the true church.

Protestant understanding of the church focuses on the preaching and teaching of the apostles rather than on any office which would secure and maintain that witness.[2] It also identifies the church with the people themselves rather than an office. For example, the Augsburg Confession, principal confessional document of the Lutheran Church, identifies the church as the congregation of believers *(communio sanctorum)*, with authenticity expressed in the presence of the Word which is purely taught and the sacraments which are rightly administered. It is the continuity of faith that is important to Protestantism, a faith that tends to be identified with correct doctrine or orthodoxy. Rather than to bestow ultimate power upon a particular office in determining orthodoxy, Protestants usually function in more democratic fashion by having their elected representatives address matters of theological importance at their church assemblies or conventions.

One of the important contributions of Vatican II in establishing new theological directions for Roman Catholicism was the Council's reference to the church as "the people of God." This image has resulted in a more "people-centered" church, giving tremendous impetus to the lay movement by providing the laity with an opportunity for greater involvement and leadership in the church. Naturally this development has not occurred without growing pains and considerable resistance. It constitutes an important route of convergence between Catholics and Protestants. The papacy itself tends to be understood in less monarchic fashion, with the Pope's decisions expected to reflect the consensus of the church at large through the counsel of the bishops.

The organization of the church in Protestantism has tended to follow one of three patterns: episcopal, presbyterian, or congregational. In episcopal churches the office of bishop is of course the primary office, but without any one bishop being given the supremacy or infallibility attributed to the papacy. Presbyterianism involves government by elders who are elected by the church at various levels of authority. Congregationalism maintains the primary importance of the local congregation as the assembly of believers and gives varying degrees of autonomy to the congregation as the actual church. Theological grounds are given for following each of these patterns of church organization, and there have been divisions as a result of theological differences over church polity.

However, the primary identifying mark of the church for Protestants has been the confession of faith in Jesus Christ and faithfulness to his lordship.

Often in these pages we have referred to "the church," and the question arises how to relate the church to the many different churches that exist. The answer of Catholics and Protestants to this question has differed. Catholics have identified the authentic church with the Roman Catholic Church because of its continuity with the apostles through apostolic succession, or the unbroken line of connection with the apostles through the bishops who followed them down to the present day. Since Vatican II non-Catholic Christians have been recognized as belonging to Christian churches, but their communions are regarded as defective in their failure to be a part of the Roman church and consequently sharing in its unity, holiness, universality and apostolicity.

Protestantism has not identified the church with any particular denomination, but has rather regarded the true church as transcending denominational lines. The church is known to God alone. The notion of an invisible church above and beyond the visible churches has often been used in Protestant thought, but it carries the obvious danger of denigrating the empirical churches and creating a spiritual ideal for a church which is not to be found anywhere on earth. On the contrary, the true church is to be found in the flesh-and-blood churches of the world where Jesus Christ is confessed in word and deed.

The question is often raised whether Jesus himself had any intention to found a church remotely resembling the actual development that has taken place. It would be wrong to claim that Jesus founded the church as it is represented by any one particular church today, or that he intended the development that has occurred. On the other hand, the very nature of his mission involved the creation of a community that would be faithful to him. His mission brought people together to share in that mission and to share it with others. With his death and resurrection the nature of that mission was both continued and transformed into something far beyond the reach of his historical ministry. The church, with all its imperfections, is the means by which his mission is communicated and enacted throughout the world. The institutional features of that community may at times be offensive (and some aspects of institutionalism in the church are inexcusable!), but such features will also be necessary for the sake of community. From a Christian point of view, there is no fellowship with God in isolation. To know God is not only to know myself, but to recognize my neighbor as one who is united with me in a common destiny prefigured by Christ. That is the basis for community at its deepest level.

At the beginning of this discussion of the marks of the church—its unity, holiness, catholicity and apostolicity—we asked whether the church is for real. In response to that question we have been compelled to recognize the ambiguity of the church. It is necessary to distinguish between the church as it is called to be by the Gospel it proclaims and the church as it really is, constituted by human beings with all their failings and lack of commitment. The Christian can only *believe* in "the holy, catholic church, the communion of saints." At the same time there is a real life of community in the name of Christ which is experienced by Christians, a life lived together under the sign of the cross. Too often, unfortunately, Christians fail to share significantly in that life together. It is a life of radical truthfulness where one experiences with others a common recognition of the deepest realities of life—our mortality, our sinfulness, our thankful dependence upon the grace of God. This kind of community is created by the Spirit, the presence of God in our lives. It provides the basis for the Christian's confidence in the ultimate vindication of the church as that community which points to —and to some degree even embodies—the destiny of human existence.

While on the way to that destiny which embraces not only the human story but the whole of creation, the church is continually reminded of its dependence upon the grace of God. One expression of this dependence is the Reformation truth, *ecclesia semper reformanda* (the church is always in need of reform). This means that the life of the church must be constantly renewed in the presence of God. The church is subject to struggle and temptation, just as the individual Christian, and it constantly needs to hear the Word of judgment as well as the Word of hope and consolation. Christians need to experience a "divine discontent" concerning the church, at the same time as they share responsibility for the church. The message of reform rightly begins with each Christian at the same time as it is directed to the church as a whole. For the individual as well as the community, it must never be forgotten that the church does not possess the Gospel to which it witnesses; it is called rather to *be* possessed by that Gospel.

The Church at Worship

Worship is not a subject that deeply moves a person living in a cultural environment as secularized as our own. A sense of awe before the majesty of God may have been close to the thoughts and feelings of people living in a previous age, but not for people in our own times. The human race itself has attained such feats of creativity and accomplishment that most expressions of awe are directed toward ourselves rather than God. Yet it is clear that a sense of mystery concerning the meaning of things still haunts the reflective person today, and for many the possibility of worship is one that is ardently desired if only they could muster the conviction to do so. Christian worship is inspired by the conviction that the awesome mystery of God is revealed in the name of "Father," with the meaning given to that name by the ministry, the death and the resurrection of Jesus Christ. Thus Christian worship takes place under the explicit confession of faith in the triune God, or "In the name of the Father, Son, and Holy Spirit."

Worship rightly understood is no peripheral activity. It brings us to the very center of our existence as beings created in the image of God. Worship is our response to God in which we recognize and give expression to the purpose and destiny of our lives. It helps us to bring focus to God in his relation to us, a relation which the Christian message conveys in the realities of both judgment and grace. Thus worship involves penitence in which we are moved to be honest with ourselves and bare our souls in the presence of God. But worship also involves praise and thanksgiving as we hear the forgiving and reconciling Word and are enabled to affirm ourselves in our acceptance by God. Our discussion of Christian worship will center on the proclamation of the Word and sacramental action as its two principal forms, as well as the implications of worship for the Christian life.

The Word and Sacraments

Because worship in the Christian congregation is shaped by trust in the triune God, there is a particular character to that worship. It is not marked primarily by meditation or silent contemplation, though of course there are appropriate times for that in the Christian life. It is not kneeling in awe before the great Unknown, and it is not communing with oneself within an aura of mystery. The triune God is the mystery revealed in its hiddenness, which means that God is no longer unknown even as God remains the ultimate mystery. Because God is known in Christ, Christian worship places the proclamation and celebration of that Word at the very center of its worship.

Protestant worship has emphasized in particular the proclamation of the Word of God in the form of the sermon. This practice goes back to the Reformation when Martin Luther saw the need of interpreting the Gospel to the uneducated masses. The worship of the people was severely threatened by many superstitious ideas as they observed holy actions from a distance, conducted in the unknown "holy language" of Latin. Today, though there always remains considerable ignorance and misunderstanding about the Gospel, people are being addressed and entertained from many different directions and the prospect of listening to yet another message on Sunday morning is not all that appealing. More important, perhaps, is that any form of public speaking meets with less patience in a time when people expect to be actively involved or at least entertained rather than to listen passively. Then there are the perennial problems of ill-prepared sermons and pastors whose talents do not include preaching, reminding us of President Woodrow Wilson's comment: "One of the proofs of the divinity of our Gospel is the preaching it has survived."

Despite these problems, the proclamation of the Word of God has something going for it that accounts for its persistence in worship. The sermon rightly understood is not to be a lecture or a talk of the pastor about ideas of his own choosing.³ Good and effective preaching is expository preaching, unfolding the meaning of scriptural texts. The preacher must be guided by the text, relating its message to the human situation so that a substantive message is conveyed which brings God and human life together. Such preaching is likely to be edifying to the congregation (which must recognize its own obligation to respond attentively!) because there is always a rich content to be mined in the scripture. The text may lend itself to a sermon which exhorts the congregation, or consoles, or nurtures, or inspires. It is not the preacher's message, but the Word of God communicated through his own words and personality. The Word proclaimed is a means of grace that conveys the reconciling love of God to the person who hears it.

In addition to the Word proclaimed there is the Word enacted, or the Word as a means of grace which is conveyed through particular actions and not just by the spoken word. This is what we mean by a sacrament, which was defined by Augustine as the Word made visible, or the Word seen and not just heard. One can speak about the cross of Jesus Christ, but one can also take bread and wine and portray his death and its meaning for us as these elements become his broken body and shed blood in the sacramental action. The sacrament of worship is variously named the Sacrament of the Altar, the Eucharist, Holy Communion, the Lord's Supper, or the Lord's Table. It is the central act of Roman Catholic worship, or the Mass, while most Protestants incorporate it only periodically in their worship. The Protestant conviction is that Word and sacrament belong together, but most Protestant worship fails to do this in actual practice since the principal emphasis falls upon the spoken word rather than the sacramental action.

The Eucharist (from the Greek word meaning "to give thanks") is a tremendously rich sacrament whose many dimensions we cannot begin to discuss. It clearly expresses the corporate character of worship, bringing people together at the altar (table) and relating them to each other as well as to the crucified Lord. It is one particular form of worship which expresses most powerfully the character of the church as the body of Christ, for at the Lord's Table the congregation reenacts the suffering and death of the incarnate

Lord and shares in his life that was offered up as it takes the sacramental host to itself. There are also the temporal dimensions of past, present and future embodied in this act. It is a remembering of Jesus from the distant past, it anticipates the ultimate fulfillment of his work in the future of God, and it brings the reality of his death and resurrection into the present as a means of grace. It is the sacrament of nurture and growth, being the one sacrament which is continuously participated in by all Christians as a means of both sharing in the benefits of Christ and uniting themselves with him in the continuation of his ministry.

This sacrament has been the center of much theological debate and divisiveness, a tragic contradiction in view of its meaning as a communal act of reconciliation. On the other hand, it is an indication of its importance that the churches have taken it so seriously in hammering out its theological meaning. The principal debate has focused on the concept of the real presence of Jesus Christ in the sacrament, a notion which has not only divided Catholics from Protestants but also Protestants from each other. The point at issue behind all the discussion of Christ's presence is whether this sacrament is a means of grace, bestowing the blessings of God's act in Christ to those who participate in it, or whether it is a memorial ceremony of the congregation in which they recall a past event for their mutual edification. Those who hold the latter view often hesitate to call the act a sacrament (preferring instead a term like "ordinance") because of suspicion about the magical connotations of that word. For them it is an act of remembering rather than the celebration of a "sacramental presence."

Though this distinction is the primary one, there remain divisions among the churches which maintain a sacramental presence over how to understand that presence. Roman Catholicism has identified the real presence of Christ with Thomas Aquinas' view of transubstantiation, which would account for Christ's presence in the bread and wine by asserting that the "substance" or the reality of the bread and wine are changed into Christ's body and blood when the priest consecrates those elements during the Mass. Though the substance has changed, the appearance or accidental characteristics remain the same, meaning that the physical elements still look and taste like bread and wine. Thomas was using the metaphysics of Aristotle which divides everything into its substance and accidents, or essence and appearances. Though he himself maintained that the sacrament is a sign, his view of transubstantiation was interpreted as a means of accounting for the actual transformation of the elements into Christ's own flesh and blood. Thus a sophisticated philosophical explanation became the basis for the Roman Church's position that Holy Communion involves a miraculous event.

The reformers, John Calvin and Martin Luther, reacted each in his own way to the realism of the Catholic understanding. To Calvin it was clear that we are dealing in the sacrament with the nourishment of the soul. Christ's presence is not within the elements, which are symbols, but a spiritual presence which is the only "real" presence we can talk about. Luther attempted to take the realism of the Catholic position more seriously than did Calvin, but found it difficult indeed to pick his way between the realist and spiritualist understandings. He spoke of Christ's presence as being "in, with, and under" the elements, leading others to identify his view as *consubstantiation* over against the Roman view of *transubstantiation*. Actually Luther wanted to move away from these Aristotelian categories and simply acknowledge a sacramental union of Christ with the elements which is unique to the sacrament and beyond our comprehension.

During recent decades theologians of all traditions have been attempting to reunderstand the sacramental presence. The ecumenical movement has been an impetus towards this reunderstanding, for new categories can result in overcoming the theological divisions of the past. In Roman Catholicism the outmoded metaphysics of Thomism has led theologians to translate transubstantiation into different categories which provide fresh interpretation of the real presence. Both Catholic and Protestant theologians are shifting the focus of Christ's presence from an exclusive preoccupation with the elements to the larger context of the sacramental action. We must remember that the primary issue concerning the Lord's Supper is whether it is a means of grace, i.e. an action in which the benefits of Christ's death on the cross are conveyed to the believer in his participation in the sacrament. Differences over how to understand Christ's presence can be accepted without denial of this more fundamental point, which involves the definition of a sacrament. If it is the Word (Jesus Christ) made visible, then it is a means of grace.

While the Sacrament of the Altar is the sacrament of corporate worship and of nurture, baptism is the sacrament of initiation which stands at the beginning of one's Christian life. Churches which do not have a strong sacramental heritage make baptism an act which follows a person's decision of faith. It is a sign and seal of one's commitment to Christ, meaning it is administered exclusively to adults. Most churches practice infant baptism, which expresses in graphic fashion that the act is a means of grace. Baptism stands at the beginning of one's life, a sign of the love of God which reaches out to all people. Baptism is a covenantal act, which means that not only is the sign of the cross placed over those being baptized but they are called to live in response to that cross. There is, once again, both gift and task involved in baptism. The baptismal covenant is renewed every time one hears the Word of God or participates at the Lord's Table, and responds to Word and sacrament with a life of faithfulness.

Baptism and the Lord's Supper are the two sacraments of Protestantism, while Roman Catholicism has five others, or a total of seven. Protestants restrict the number to two by insisting that a genuine sacrament must have been instituted or specifically commanded by Jesus. Their definition of a sacrament also includes the use of a material substance and the bestowal of grace. Catholics, on the other hand, see the sacraments as the church's opportunity to celebrate and bring a redemptive sign to the important events or moments of our lives. Thus confirmation is a sacrament, as well as marriage, the consecration of priests, penance, and extreme unction (for the gravely ill). Many Protestants would be willing to recognize the sacramental character of these acts, even if they do not regard them as sacraments.

We make one final observation concerning the difference in character between Roman Catholic and Protestant worship. The worship of Catholicism impresses the Protestant with its strong visual character. There is much to be seen in the elaborate ritual, the colorful vestments, and the sacramental action which is replete with symbolic gestures. Protestant worship, in emphasizing the spoken word rather than sacramental action, is focused more towards hearing than seeing. Protestants generally do not have the same appreciation for the symbolic act; they are used to the message being verbalized and consequently there is a more intellectual or rational temper to many Protestant services. This difference between the visual and auditory mode is further reflected in the aesthetic dimensions of worship in each of these traditions. Catholicism makes much more use of the visual arts (paintings, sculpture, etc.) while it is no accident that the Reformation brought a rebirth of music in the church, the art to which one listens. Music also affords Protestant worshipers the opportunity to participate in the service as a corporate group, a development which was appropriate to the Protestant understanding of the church as the congregation of believers.

Worship and the Kingdom of God

Many Christians tend to think of worship as a religious activity conducted in church, with no integral relation to the rest of their lives. People who no longer go to church usually regard the essence of religion to be the moral life, and in many cases they have left the church precisely because worship has appeared irrelevant to the more important business of living that life. These views may be understandable in light of the usual practice in Christian congregations, but they are deplorable to one who perceives the meaning of Christian worship.

One avenue in getting at the fullness of that meaning is to consider the word *liturgy*. This word, which is used to denote forms of worship in the church, has its origin in the realm of municipal affairs, or local politics. It comes from the Greek word, *leitourgia*, which means "a work of the people." In the Christian context it came to denote the communal act or "work" of worship, specifically the Sacrament of the Altar. There are powerful implications involved in this sacrament which break the artificial boundaries we place around it, leading us back to politics and the world of the marketplace. In Holy Communion we take bread and wine, two staples of human existence, and consecrate them to a holy use. They become the broken body and shed blood of Christ, redemptive signs which not only convey the benefits of Christ's cross but point to the destiny of the whole creation. This is so because the bread and wine are samples of the material and social order in which we live, products of both the earth and of human industry. The secular is made holy in this act; the church is not removed from the world in worship, but consecrates the world by placing it under the cross of Christ.

In other words, Christian worship expresses the responsibility of the church for the world in which it lives. While the church at worship is the congregation of believers, that worship turns the church to the world in the spirit of Jesus Christ whose ministry was one of healing and reconciliation. Jesus identifies his own ministry by referring to the Servant Songs in Isaiah:

> The Spirit of the Lord God is upon me, because the Lord has anointed me to bring good tidings to the afflicted; he has sent me to bind up the brokenhearted, to proclaim liberty to the captives, and the opening of the prison to those who are bound . . . (Isa. 61:1; cf. Luke 4:16-19).

This servant role of Jesus can be applied to the church as well. Its worship moves from the table of the Lord to the streets of the city, the homes and the marketplace. Its mission is not only to herald the good news but to embody it in a ministry of healing and reconciliation wherever the world is hurting. Salvation in its biblical meaning cannot be understood in any narrow, spiritualist sense. The church is bound by its worship to minister as it can to the whole of life.

When one speaks of the church's mission it is helpful to speak of the kingdom of God. This concept, which was integral to the message and ministry of Jesus, not only points the church to the future but helps it understand the nature of its mission here and now. The kingdom of God expresses the destiny of human existence, a destiny in God as the consummation of our lives. As we have noted, Jesus Christ prefigures that destiny for us in his resurrection, and directs us toward it as well in his ministry. The church not only shares in that ministry when it carries out its work of healing and reconciliation. It also directs the world toward its proper destiny, the kingdom of God. The church is not the kingdom itself, but in its faithfulness to its mission it becomes a sign of that kingdom for the nations. The universality of the kingdom of God reminds the church that it does not exist for itself, but for the world. The church's mission is to lose itself in the service of humankind.

Whether in worship or in ministry, the church is responding to the sovereignty of God which is expressed in the language of the kingdom. It is true to itself when it confesses and celebrates that sovereignty in worship, and when it is obedient to that sovereignty in mission. But God's sovereignty, while recognized by faith, will not arrive at its own completion until "the day of Jesus Christ," the eschaton. Thus there is a forward-directed motion to the church's life at the same time as it is conscious of its apostolic heritage out of the past. The apostolic message conveys the promise which is to be ultimately realized in the future of God.

9

On Being Faithful

IN THE OPENING PAGES OF THIS BOOK we discussed the presence and necessity of faith in human life, and the character of Christian faith as one option among many that invites the commitment of people today. We have emphasized the fact that Christian faith is an invitation to a life-commitment, based on the conviction that God is acting in our world. This means that Christian faith involves certain convictions about God and his relation to human beings, convictions which we have discussed in the chapters that followed. These convictions are the "deposit of faith," or that which is believed and which has been passed on through the centuries in the witness and teaching of the church. To affirm these convictions is at the same time to respond with one's life to the invitation of God that is implicit in them. In other words, to believe that Jesus Christ is God's Word to the human race is to recognize Jesus as one's Lord and strive to be faithful to him. The bottom line in Christian faith is one's trust in Jesus, or one's devotion to him.

Thus we conclude our consideration of an "invitation to faith" by noting in this chapter some dimensions of a faithful life. We shall discuss first the struggle of faith involving one's personal life of conviction and devotion, and then the adventure of faith that involves one's life in relationship with others, or life in society.

Problems in Personal Commitment

The problems that people encounter in living the Christian life are as varied as each individual himself. Yet there are problems that are common to most Christians. One of those problems is the gnawing presence of doubt. For anyone who reflects on the Christian message it is hardly conceivable that doubts would not arise. Particularly during high school and college years the Christian is made aware of knowledge or philosophical views which challenge Christian belief. Another subject often discussed as a problem in recent times is prayer. Because of its vital importance to the Christian life, problems concerning prayer often get at the heart of faith itself. In considering problems of one's personal life of faith, we shall focus on these two subjects.

Dealing with Doubt

Doubt cannot be regarded as simply a negative concept. On the contrary, it is usually an expression of honesty in the believer. If every doubt were simply suppressed, it would be no victory for faith. Quite often in the history of the church there have been attempts to insulate faith from the probing intellect, but the church is always the loser whenever this happens. Roman Catholic theologians speak quite openly now about the unfortunate attempts of their church during the nineteenth century to insulate itself from every viewpoint in contemporary culture that would raise doubts in the minds of the faithful. We have noted in Chapter 2 that both Protestant and Catholic churches have attempted to create a security for faith by ascribing divine attributes to their sources of authority (the Bible and the papacy). As long as one remains a dutiful believer of the church who accepts everything without question, this system can work. But what kind of faith is that?

Søren Kierkegaard makes a helpful distinction between "childlike" and "childish" faith. There is the quality of the child in every person who professes Christian faith, regardless how old or wise or formidable that person may be. But a childlike faith, expressed in simple trust and confidence, does not mean that faith is childish. The latter occurs whenever adults attempt to believe as though they were children, refusing to allow their adult consciousness to recognize and seriously examine the meaning and implications of their faith. It results in a simplistic kind of faith, oblivious of every challenge or question that is raised. Paul Tillich points out that a self-critical principle is at work in the Reformation expression of Christian faith, a principle which is inherent to the Gospel itself. It compels us to question every attempt to make our faith secure, removing the venture and risk that are integral to faith. That critical principle involves the willingness to question and to doubt every human expression of ultimacy in our religion.

Thus we can appreciate the cleansing, purifying function of doubt as an expression of honesty in the life of faith, and we can recognize it also as the natural expression of growth from childhood to maturity in one's faith-life. We can, furthermore, recognize that so fundamental an act of faith as affirming the reality of God can never be free from disturbing challenges. In view of the many absurdities and tragedies of life, perhaps the greatest problem one has with the good news of God revealed in Jesus Christ is that it is too good to be true. But there remains the question whether there is not finally a point at which one *can* no longer doubt. Are there not certain essential affirmations in the Christian confession which to doubt would be to reject the God of the Gospel? This would be doubt which leads one to despair of the truth of the Christian message. Doubt in its ultimate form is despair.

What then would be the vital core of Christian faith, which to doubt would bring one to despair? In view of what we have said in these pages, it would have to do with Jesus himself. Is he or is he not the clue to the meaning of things, the "human face of God" whose life and message, whose death and resurrection point us to the living God? Jesus Christ as "God with us" is the anchor of Christian faith; to lose this anchor is to be set adrift from the good news that his life embodies. The church's theology may well not be correct in many of its doctrinal formulations concerning Jesus, but in regard to the ultimate meaning of his life, does he or does he not reveal God to us—the God of love in whom we can trust? Paul locates the crucial issue concerning the meaning of Jesus in the resurrection: ". . . if Christ has not been raised, then our preaching is in vain and your faith is in vain" (1 Cor. 15:14). Without the crucified and risen Christ, the Christian would have no reason to hope. The last word would not be the resurrection, but at best the verdict of Albert Camus who speaks of "the benign indifference of the universe."

There is another important dimension to the problem of doubt. Because faith is not just an act of the intellect but a commitment of the whole person, is it not a mistake to suppose that doubt arises exclusively from a questioning intellect? Doubt may be an expression of one's unwillingness to make the kind of commitment entailed by trust in Jesus Christ. To believe is to obey, to subject oneself to a sensitized conscience, to reach out in a spirit of love to one's neighbor. That may be reason enough to raise questions about the Christian faith! It is too idealistic, too demanding of a compassionate and understanding heart to be taken seriously. Pascal was convinced that the difficulty posed by obedience was the primary obstacle to Christian faith. On the other hand, perhaps more doubt of this kind is needed, for it at least takes seriously the ethical demand of Christian commitment.

How Does One Pray?

In our discussion of the Christian understanding of God we recognized the necessity of speaking of God in personal terms.[1] In Christ God confronts us as "Thou"; personal language best conveys the reality of God who is revealed in the life, death and resurrection of Jesus. That revelation brings the conviction that God addresses us in the events and circumstances of our lives in which we are called to account and in which our lives are renewed and restored in the experience of grace. This character of Christian faith makes prayer both natural and necessary.

Prayer is the response of the believer to this presence of God in one's life. But God's presence is not a tangible thing. God does not intrude upon our lives as *a* person, so that we are aware of God in the same way that we are aware of other people. Thus prayer is not communication in the sense of two people speaking to each other, even though the Christian imagination may often picture it this way. Many problems that people have with prayer are based on this misconception, for their understanding of God as a person leads them to expect an answer to prayer which would be appropriate to one person responding to another. But we know it does not work that way, in spite of a certain kind of Christian piety that expresses sweet thoughts about the garden in which one "walks" and "talks" with God. The mystery of God cannot be dissolved by such language.

To pray is to open oneself to the lordship or sovereignty of God, acknowledging his presence and his purpose for us. It is not surprising that Paul speaks of prayer in conjunction with the Spirit, for prayer is the response of those who have been moved by the presence of God to express their deepest aspirations. It may be a prayer of thanksgiving, or confession of sin, or intercession in behalf of someone else, or a prayer of petition. But whatever the form of prayer, it is an act of worship in which people acknowledge their dependence and express their trust in God. This is done together with other Christians in congregational worship, and the forms used by the congregation—whether derived from the Bible (particularly the Psalms) or from the riches of the church's devotional literature down through the ages—provide a tremendous resource for individuals in their own prayer life.

The criticism directed by the so-called secular theologians against Christian theism has carried with it a questioning attitude about prayer as an activity of the inner life. The point is made that prayer as withdrawal from the world is not an appealing or effective activity for Christians today. Just as God is found in the marketplace as well as in holy places, so prayer is no holy activity in isolation from the world. It is redefined in terms of living faithfully in the world, or as the consecrated activity of the Christian who works for peace and justice in society. While this view is commendable in its identifying of prayer with one's whole life lived in responsibility to the Gospel, prayer is still a distinctive activity within the life of faith. It is an act of faith in which one's life is consciously presented to God, whether in an expression of thanksgiving, confession, intercession or petition.

It is these last two forms of prayer, intercession and petition, which pose the real problem for our understanding of prayer. We have maintained that prayer is not talking to God as to another person. Thus we do not rightly expect God to miraculously heal a friend dying of cancer, or to provide food for the people starving in the Third World. As Bonhoeffer pointed out, we look to human resources to cope with our problems rather than expecting miraculous solutions. What then is the alternative? Do we refrain from praying in such situations? Are prayers of petition simply exercises in futility, helpful perhaps as a cathartic expression for one's own subjectivity but not to be regarded as real requests for real solutions? This is one possible conclusion, but it is not the conclusion of Christian faith.

In our discussion of divine providence we noted that this concept is not to be understood as though God were a giant who is in total control of all that happens, pulling the strings as he sees fit. Our image of God is informed by Jesus Christ, whose life is marked by suffering love and whose destiny was resurrection on the other side of this life. In view of this conviction we can say that petitions of faith are heard by One who does not intrude miraculously in human affairs in response to our requests, but takes to himself the pain and agony of his children and promises a new life—a resurrected life—in our future. Things are not made right in the present, but the Gospel nonetheless brings an answer to our petitions which turns us to the future in hope. Thus there is an eschatological character to prayer. We can respond to Jesus' command to bring one's requests to the Father, not with the expectation that everything will be worked out to our satisfaction (even when our desires have been cleansed of selfish motivations!), but rather with the expectation that in God our lives and the whole of creation will find their completion. Thus our prayers of petition and intercession can and should always be united with the thankful expression, "Thy will be done."

How then does one pray? There is no one way to pray, but when the Gospel touches our lives so that we are moved to respond to its message, prayer is one way in which we respond. It is the utterance of one who is grateful, or the sorrow of one who is contrite, or the plea of one who is concerned and perhaps struggling. The spirit of Christian prayer is governed by the cross and resurrection, which means that prayer unites us with suffering wherever it is found and at the same time expresses a hope which comes not from ourselves but from the Gospel. Such prayer is not selfish, even though it may express our needs. It is honest prayer, which places our own situation in proper perspective and acknowledges our dependence on God.

The Faithful Life

If faith is commitment and trust, as we have asserted several times, then the life of faith is the life of faithfulness. To believe is to obey. This involves our lives in relation to others and to society at large, for it is in the arena of human relationships that we are provided the opportunity and the responsibility for living out our response to the Gospel. Human relationships introduce the world of values or morality, that pervasive sphere of life in which we demonstrate to the world what kind of people we are. Our purpose here is not to discuss specific moral issues in our society in view of Christian principles, but to consider briefly the basis for a Christian ethic, or a Christian response to the world of human relationships.

The Ethics of Love

Where does one turn to find the source of Christian ethics, or the guidelines for responsible Christian living in today's world? We noted in the previous chapter that among the variety of churches there is a variety of moralities with some churches far more restrictive than others concerning what is acceptable Christian behavior. Christian theologians argue whether there is in fact a specifically *Christian* ethic at all. When we asked in Chapter 1 about the uniqueness of the Christian faith we pointed to Jesus as the one who gives the distinctive content to that faith. One would have to draw the same conclusion concerning Christian ethics. Not only the ethical teachings of Jesus but the mission and character of his life provide the Christian with the foundation for Christian ethics.[2]

Central to Jesus' teaching is the kingdom of God, which we have understood as the rule or reign of God. Jesus speaks of the kingdom in both present and future terms, associating God's rule with himself but also looking forward to its coming. This anticipation of the kingdom gives a strong eschatological character to Jesus' teaching, which means that his ethical teaching turns us to the future for the realization of God's reign. The proper response to the coming kingdom is repentance and faith: "The time is fulfilled, and the kingdom of God is at hand; repent, and believe in the gospel" (Mark 1:15). This is a call to radical obedience which Jesus does not present in any systematic, detailed fashion but paints in bold, broad strokes. It is essentially a call to love, which Jesus regards as the fundamental imperative expressed in the moral laws of his people.

> And one of them, a lawyer, asked him a question, to test him. "Teacher, which is the great commandment in the law?" And he said to him, "You shall love the Lord your God with all your heart, and with all your soul, and with all your mind. This is the great and first commandment. And a second is like it, You shall love your neighbor as yourself. On these two commandments depend all the law and the prophets" (Matt. 22:35-40).

Jesus' ethic of love is rooted in the love of God the Father, which means that love is not simply an abstract ideal. God the Father is the source and motivation for a life of love which transforms the commonsense ethic of self-interest to an ethic of self-giving love:

> You have heard that it was said, "You shall love your neighbor and hate your enemy." But I say to you, Love your enemies and pray for those who persecute you, so that you may be sons of your Father who is in heaven; for he makes his sun rise on the evil and on the good, and sends rain on the just and on the unjust (Matt. 5:43-45).

The picture of God the Father presented in Jesus' teaching is so vital and personal that he becomes the moving power behind the life of faith. The love of God is expressed both in creative, providential acts as well as in the restoration and forgiveness of the fallen, as in the parable of the prodigal son (Luke 15). We are exhorted to be perfect as our heavenly Father is perfect (Matt. 5:48), a perfection which can be expressed as the wholeness of perfect love.

It is a love which moves us to go the second mile, to sacrifice beyond the call of duty (Matt. 5:38-42).

One must remember that Jesus is speaking of the Old Testament law when he sums up its meaning in terms of love. He is not giving us such a radically new ethic that it has no relation to the tradition of the Jews. In fact most of his ethical injunctions have their parallels in the rabbinic literature. But Jesus' picture of God the Father as loving and compassionate results in an unusually powerful ethic of sacrificial love. He cuts through the legalism of rabbinic teaching to present the demands of discipleship with a boldness and freshness unparalleled in the tradition of his fathers.

Christian ethics, however, is more than Jesus' ethical teaching. Jesus Christ himself was seen by New Testament writers as the embodiment of divine love in the human story, the result being an ethic based on Christ as God's sign of sacrificial love in the world:

> Beloved, let us love one another; for love is of God, and he who loves is born of God and knows God. He who does not love does not know God; for God is love. In this the love of God was made manifest among us, that God sent his only Son into the world, so that we might live through him. In this is love, not that we loved God but that he loved us and sent his Son to be the expiation for our sins. Beloved, if God so loved us, we also ought to love one another (1 John 4:7-11).

Not only the meaning of Jesus Christ as God's gift, but also Jesus' own life of obedience to the Father becomes the ground for Christian exhortation:

> Have this mind among yourselves, which is yours in Christ Jesus, who, though he was in the form of God, did not count equality with God a thing to be grasped, but emptied himself, taking the form of a servant, being born in the likeness of men. And being found in human form he humbled himself and became obedient unto death, even death on a cross (Phil. 2:5-8).

Clearly, love is no abstract ideal in Christian ethics. Jesus himself is the flesh and blood standard of what love means in terms of sacrificial living. His own life led him to the cross, which has become the Christian symbol of suffering love. The term used by New Testament writers to express this self-giving love is *agape,* or love which gives without seeking something in return. Other words were used in the Greek language to express erotic love, or the attraction between the sexes, as well as the love expressed in the bond of friendship, or brotherly and sisterly love. Agapeic love is distinctive in its being rooted in God, conveying a message of grace as well as an imperative to move out from the bonds of self-interest and to love our neighbor as we have been loved.

The question has often been raised whether this ethic of love is not so exalted and demanding as to be irrelevant. Are there not legitimate self-interests which prevent us from going the second mile, or which justify our refusing to turn the other cheek or to offer up our cloak when our coat has been taken? What about obligations to our family which prevent us from meeting the needs of our neighbor? The $500 I have in my bank account may be desperately needed by my neighbor, but don't my wife and children have a prior claim to that money since it is all I have? It is our experience of these competing claims that often makes ethics a difficult and complicated business. Yet it is precisely these competing ethical claims that Jesus does not consider. In the eschatological urgency of the kingdom, we are placed in a one-to-one relationship with our neighbor who is in need. Nothing else matters but the need of our neighbor, and we are challenged to respond to it in a spirit of sacrifice.

Though this uncompromising demand of love may appear to be far removed from the realities of life as we experience them, it is actually this very radicality which gives the Christian ethic its enduring power. The ethic of agapeic love challenges the self-centered character of our conduct, inviting us to take the adventure of selfless living. It involves the spirit of our actions, challenging us to rigorous self-criticism and to take seriously the situation of our neighbor. But most importantly it places before us the figure of Jesus Christ as the one who demonstrates in his own life just what it means to be motivated by love. The quiet strength of his own character and person is a testimony to the power of love in a person's life. The servanthood of Jesus issued not from weakness but from strength. It was a servanthood freely chosen, directed by the spirit of obedient love. As such, his life constitutes an example which transcends the ages, inviting his followers to let that same spirit of compassion rule their own lives.

One way in which this demanding ethic is expressed is in Jesus' words about losing one's life in order to find it, or giving oneself to others as the way of receiving oneself. Blessing is found in feeding the hungry, caring for the afflicted, ministering to the needs of others—not as a means of gaining self-fulfillment but as a work of love which is its own reward. Both corporately and individually, the Christian community is called to die to itself, living the life of sacrificial action. In an age when society is obsessed with an often superficial pursuit of self-fulfillment, the Christian ethic challenges one to a life of suffering. Yet how far removed is this idea from the thinking that is often found within the church, where people like to associate the Christian life with material rewards which are seen as tangible evidences of God's favor. The absurdity of this view is driven home in the wry comment of Samuel Butler: "To love God is to have good health, good looks, good luck, and a fair balance of cash in the bank."

The Ethics of Freedom

It must be understood when discussing Christian ethics that it is an ethics of faith. It is not a set of rules that provides an ethical code for anyone who might decide to abide by that code. It is grounded on the Gospel message, which means that it is an orientation toward life in which one acknowledges one's dependence on God's grace in Christ and is moved by that divine acceptance to live a life of grateful response. "We love, because he first loved us" (1 John 4:19). The Sermon on the Mount (Matt. 5-7) is not moral legislation for society at large, but rather depicts an orientation toward life for those who have responded to the call, "Repent and believe!" and have dedicated themselves to a life of discipleship. The radical character of the imperatives in the Sermon on the

Mount should make it clear that Jesus is speaking to those who have identified with the coming kingdom.

When the apostles related God's rule to the event of Jesus Christ, their understanding of the moral life became rooted in Jesus as the deed of God on our behalf. It was particularly Paul who emphasized that consequently the Christian's moral life is not designed to gain the favor of God, or to achieve one's salvation through the performance of good works. This would be the ethics of law, which he identifies from his own experience with Judaism and which he contrasts with the ethics of the Gospel. The ethics of law exercises a bondage over the individual according to the seriousness with which one devotes oneself to it. The more serious one becomes about observing the law, the more demanding the law becomes. If one believes that observance of the law is the pathway to God's favor, then one becomes serious indeed. The result is an ethics of bondage, for the law becomes a taskmaster which is never satisfied.

The ethics of the Gospel is characterized by Paul as an ethics of freedom. "For freedom Christ has set us free; stand fast therefore, and do not submit again to a yoke of slavery" (Gal. 5:1). The Christian need no longer use the law as a ladder to heaven. God's deed in Christ removes every need for self-justification before God or anyone else. It is God who makes us righteous (acceptable), not we ourselves. This fact has a liberating effect because it locates the promise of our present and future in God rather than ourselves, thus giving us the basis for hope and confidence that we ourselves could not produce. Furthermore, without having to *earn* anything by exemplary behavior, we are free to respond to the needs of the world as God has blessed us.

Among the Protestant reformers it was Luther who experienced a particular kinship with the apostle Paul. Burdened as he was by the legalism of the medieval church, he was personally liberated by the Pauline message of justification by grace through faith. He magnified divine grace in his doctrine of justification, stressed "the freedom of the Christian man" in his tract by that title, and contrasted the Gospel with the law of God whose principal function was to indict, or bring one to an awareness of one's sin. As in

Paul, law and Gospel were regarded basically as antitheses. The Christian life is best characterized as "faith working through love" (Gal. 5:6b) rather than a life lived according to the law.

One encounters a different atmosphere in the ethics of John Calvin. While stressing with Luther the foundation of grace in the Christian life, Calvin was more intent on developing the Christian community. This meant, as we can see from his work in Geneva, that he was compelled to rely on law as the means of achieving his goal. Where Luther's theology tended to separate justification as God's act from sanctification as the process of nurture and growth, Calvin brought them together as simultaneous acts and was more inclined to understand faith in terms of rebirth and the sanctified life. Where Luther stressed "Christ for us" Calvin stressed "Christ in us;" not just the grace of God in Christ but the "law of Christ" was essential to fulfilling God's purpose for us. John Wesley, the founder of Methodism in the nineteenth century, gave further impetus to a legal understanding of the Christian life by introducing the notion of perfectibility. This had the effect of identifying Christian morality with certain moral prohibitions.

The understanding of justification and sanctification in Roman Catholic theology carries a different emphasis from that of Reformation thought. The reason for this is bound up with the difference in the view of grace. Reformation theology understands grace as the disposition of God toward us, describing the undeserved goodness of God expressed in the Gospel message. Catholic theology understands grace within the context of sacramental action, in which grace is bestowed as a charism or gift which contributes to the acceptability of the believer. In this view, justification is virtually identified with the sanctification of the sinner through sacramental grace. Law and Gospel are united in the process of sanctification, with both grace and the works of the law contributing to the redeemed life.

From the time of the apostle Paul, the idea of the freedom of the Christian life has always raised questions about what is allowable for Christians and what is not. Is the freedom of the Christian an invitation to license? Are moral laws of no importance or relevance to the Christian? Clearly Paul is not advocating moral anarchy. He is saying that the life of faith is motivated by love, and love *(agape)* constrains us to act responsibly as well as venturously. The liberating power of love could hardly lead to intentional wrong-doing; it leads to works of love. Paul speaks of these deeds as "the fruit of the Spirit" which need no law, indicating that they issue from a life open to a power greater than oneself:

> But the fruit of the Spirit is love, joy, peace, patience, kindness, goodness, faithfulness, gentleness, self-control; against such there is no law. And those who belong to Christ Jesus have crucified the flesh with its passions and desires.
>
> If we live by the Spirit, let us also walk by the Spirit (Gal. 5:22-25).

What about Situation Ethics?

The question of how to relate law and Gospel in the Christian life is at the center of the argument over situation ethics. That argument has often shed more heat than light because of wholesale misrepresentation of what is being said by situationists. On the other hand, some situationists have invited misunderstanding by overstating their case. The loaded expression, "the new morality," which tends to be identified with situation ethics, has contributed further to the general confusion. Someone has said that "the new morality is the old immorality condoned." For theologians who espouse a situationist position, this statement is not only unfair but fails to get at the point they are raising. They are asking the question, "What is the nature of Christian ethics?" In doing this they are at the same time attacking the kind of ethics which they see as prevalent in the church and which they believe fails to express the essential nature of the Christian life.[3]

We have noted the centrality of love in the ethics of the New Testament. Situationists exalt agapeic love as the essence of the Christian life, and seek to spell out the implications of this fact. One implication is that love is the one, universal absolute in Christian ethics, subordinating every moral law or rule to itself. To act in a spirit of love does not prescribe ahead of time just exactly what one ought to do. It involves a reading of the situation, getting the facts straight that define the ethical problem, and then acting in a spirit of love. To be sure, there are certain principles or guidelines for behavior that can be of help in making an ethical decision, but it is the situation itself which really determines whether loving action should follow an accepted law of conduct.

In exalting love, situationists tend to make an absolute antithesis between love and law, a characteristic we have noted in the writings of both Paul and Luther. The focal point of the discussion, however, is different. Both Paul and Luther were primarily concerned with the bondage of legalism in the religious and moral life in contrast to the freedom bestowed by the Gospel. Situationists rightly make the same point, but as the name suggests, the stress falls on the situational character of moral decision-making and the inadequacy of law in the form of universal prohibitions applied to specific situations. Each situation has its own uniqueness in terms of the people involved and the peculiarities of their personal relationships. Abstract prohibitions cannot take these situational factors into account; they simply say, "Thou shalt not. . . ."

Two points are commonly made by critics of situation ethics. One is that there are no isolated situations unrelated to the rest of our moral decision-making. Instead of beginning with the situation, we in fact begin with certain moral imperatives or ground rules which govern our behavior and provide a basis for acting responsibly upon entering a situation. In other words, we begin with the ground rules, or a pattern of acceptable behavior, not with the situation. The situation is but one factor in arriving at a moral decision, and most often it does not occasion the suspension of a ground rule. A second point is that moral laws can be expressions of love in the sense of respect for the rights of the other person. Law helps us to be faithful to others in terms of the obligations we have toward them. The real antithesis in the situation ethics debate is not love versus law but love versus legalism, or the exercise of law for the sake of law rather than for the sake of human welfare.

One salutary effect of situation ethics is that it has helped Christians to become sensitive to the danger of legalism in the church. Wherever people are religiously or morally serious, legalism is an imminent temptation. Laws of conduct are not ends in themselves but are to be used responsibly by the Christian. Usually they must be taken with absolute seriousness. Sometimes they should be subordinated to what the situation requires. But this calls for individual maturity, a point that situationists are quite willing to acknowledge. Christian ethics does presuppose repentance and faith, after all, which presumes a degree of moral seriousness and a sense of self-identity. The use of rules of behavior are of course particularly important in the nurture of the young, who have not yet sufficiently internalized moral values to insure mature conduct. Their emphasis upon love and the situation often prevents situationists from giving sufficient attention to this fact. But even for the mature Christian, the presence of a strong "Thou shalt not!" is sometimes needed to help one act responsibly.

It is a rare Christian ethicist who does not recognize the fact that the simple application of absolute rules does not do justice to the concrete situation. We cannot even take one of the Ten Commandments without imagining a situation in which breaking that commandment may well be the lesser of two evils. Are there not some situations in which it is better to lie, or necessary to kill? But this does not mean that therefore such norms are simply a matter of personal taste or custom. Our laws and commandments that protect us from the exploitation of others are profoundly important to us as expressions of our trust in the meaningfulness of human life and in values that are inherent to that life. But this does not deny that those values must be applied to concrete situations and affirmed in a way that is appropriate or relative to them. Thus it is posing false alternatives to say that one either believes in absolutes or maintains that everything is relative. Perhaps it is best to speak of the general validity of those laws or commandments which have served through the ages to maintain order in society. As such they are expressions of love in the sense of respect for one's neighbor.

Where do these observations bring us in regard to the relation of law and love in the Christian life? It would appear that there is both a negative and a positive relationship between law and love. Paul and Luther rightly contrasted the two in discerning the basis of the Christian life as a grateful response to God's love, rather than a code of law. The issue here is what *motivates* the

Christian's life of faithfulness—it is not the fear of punishment or the condemnation of the law, but the pain of faithlessness to the Father of his Lord Jesus Christ. The law can be at times a painful reminder of our weakness in living a faithful life when it calls us to account, pulling us up short and making us recognize that what we were intending to do was not a responsible act, or one motivated by love. On the other hand, law does serve in a positive way as a structure of support for faithful living. The motive of love will often move the Christian to go beyond the sense of duty conveyed by the law, but only in rare and extreme situations can one conceive of a loving action which goes contrary to the morality of law. In other words, what the law demands of us is a respect for the other person which a spirit of love would not want to deny.

What agitates many people today is their perception that respect for law in our society is eroding and that even now we are in the throes of a moral crisis. All the established mores seem to be in a state of flux, whether one speaks of marriage and family, sexual relationships, vocations and work, education, or economic and political structures. It is a temptation of concerned people at such a time to rush to the ramparts and fight for a return to the tried and true values of the past. This course of action tends to be self-defeating, however. From a Christian point of view the future is never without hope, and change that may appear threatening must be analyzed carefully for the promise that it also brings. In many ways our society has become more sensitive to injustice, and young people continue to bring a high idealism to many individual and corporate tasks. The proper Christian response to the uncertainties of our time is to evaluate critically the changes that are taking place, and support every change that seems to promise a more just and humane social order. By the same token, Christian faithfulness certainly involves speaking out against those features of mass society that dehumanize people and destroy the possibilities of meaningful human community.

We have come now from a consideration of the basis of the Christian moral life to the question of social ethics, or the Christian response to the social issues of our time. Our purpose here is not to discuss these issues but to consider one approach to the social order which has emerged in the Christian community in recent years. It is *liberation theology*, which advocates fundamental changes in the social order and has caused a lively debate among theologians.

Liberation Theology

Liberation is one of the most powerful ideas of our time, expressing deeply-felt needs and aspirations of people who are experiencing significant forms of oppression. Christians have responded to these forms of oppression by developing theologies of liberation. There are several such theologies now current in our own society, notably by and for blacks and women. The most extensive theological literature on this theme does not come from our own society, however, but from Latin America. It is a theology of liberation for the Third World which carries profoundly unsettling ideas for Christians living in North America. It is this literature on which we shall focus as an illustration of one way in which Christians today are trying to be faithful in relating their convictions to the society in which they live.

It has been estimated that if the world population of more than four billion were represented by 1,000 people, those whose lives could be regarded as both free from the scourge of hunger and the arbitrary acts of oppressive political regimes would total just 164. That number may be argued, but it is at least enough of a ballpark figure to indicate a problem which has become increasingly intense as our world has become a global village. Liberation theology begins from the conviction that the poor and oppressed must constitute the starting point of Christian theology. Not only did Jesus identify with the poor of his own time, but in every age there is no more pressing issue in relation to the church's mission and the kingdom of God than the oppressed of the earth. This is the concrete historical situation which must govern all of our theologizing.

In Latin American countries this theology has both informed and generated a growing restlessness in the church, because the church itself has long been identified with oppressive, totalitarian regimes.[4] Many priests have openly identified themselves with the poor and

have supported revolutionary movements. Camilo Torres, a de-
frocked priest who joined a revolutionary guerrilla group, was
ambushed and slain by government forces in 1966. Dom Helder
Camara, the "poor people's bishop" in Brazil, has become a folk
hero through his support of the poor and by his brave defiance of
the political and religious establishment. Liberation theology is a
theology of deed, of praxis, which means that heresy is primarily
false action, or failure to act in behalf of the kingdom of God.

> Poverty is an evil, a scandalous condition, which in our
> times has taken on enormous proportions. To eliminate it
> is to bring closer the moment of seeing God face to face, in
> union with other men.[5]

This stress on action to bring some concrete change to the plight
of the masses has convinced liberation theologians that they cannot
simply criticize the structures of oppression; they must make their
contribution toward changing them. This has led them to espouse
a sociopolitical analysis of society which could provide the basis for
concrete social change. At this point their stance becomes suspicious
and even offensive to many North American Christians, for their
analysis is Marxist. It identifies the poor with the proletarian class
and indicts capitalism as the culprit in establishing economic and
political patterns of oppression. It is of course made clear that their
use of Marxism is purely in terms of its analytic value in discerning
the ills of society, and does not involve its materialist philosophy.
But they are convinced that the Marxist analysis provides the most
promise for an accurate understanding of their situation and for
prescribing the changes that are needed.

How shall we evaluate this theology of liberation? North American and European theology has emphasized the importance of
maintaining neutrality over against political and economic pro-
grams. If theology is to be effective in its responsibility to society,
it must remain aloof from ideologies of either the left or the right,
exercising a critique of both on the basis of humanitarian concerns
for freedom and justice. For the church to be faithful to the demands of love, it must be a force for justice without being manipulated by either those who possess power or those who seek power.

Liberation theologians respond by saying that for them to maintain neutrality in their position would be irresponsible. Not only is the oppression so obvious and extreme, but the biblical mandate clearly places the Christian at the side of the poverty-stricken. Even the violence of revolution may be warranted if there is no other way to realize a just society.

It is argued, furthermore, that we who live in affluent societies are not really so non-ideological as we pretend to be. We have constructed an abstract, "privatized" humanity as the object of our theologizing, divorcing people from their concrete social environment which should provide the context for doing theology. As an illustration of this point, consider the manner in which the Gospel of Jesus Christ has been interpreted in this book. We have related that Gospel first of all to the individual person who is confronted by the existential realities of life—one's mortality, one's guilt, one's quest for meaning and a sense of destiny. To be sure, the quest for meaning moved us from the individual to the community and to the social implications of Christian faith, but these were all implications rather than immediately integral to our point of departure. Liberation theologians change the order so that one proceeds from society to the individual, emphasizing that the kingdom of God is a *social* reality that cannot be divorced from the actual conditions in which one lives. We have presented the Gospel in these pages as liberation from the bondage of sin, guilt, and the despair of meaninglessness in the face of death. Liberation theologians insist on addressing first the environmental problem of poverty, which destroys the very capacity of the human spirit to respond to questions of meaning and destiny.

Liberation theology sensitizes us in a forceful way to the fact that every effective theology is one that grows out of its historical situation and addresses that situation. To the extent that questions of meaning and destiny that transcend one's immediate environment are real to the society in which we live, a theology that addresses these very questions is communicating effectively. I suspect that these questions are not all that far removed from people in the Third World, and yet the point we can learn from liberation theologians is that meaning and destiny are not simply spiritual ideas but involve the whole person in the context of one's environment. Death and resurrection are meaningful terms by which to understand our destiny, but we must understand that death comes to us in many ways. The human spirit is assaulted and can be destroyed by the inhumanity of one's environment before one's mortal life is completed. If we do not grasp this and concern ourselves with the battle for a more just society, then resurrection itself may be no more than a selfish desire for one's own reward.

Just as our theologies are not adequate as they stand for people living in significantly different environments, so we can also conclude that a Third World theology is inadequate for us who live in North America. It is a theology for those involved in the struggle for their own liberation from oppression. But because that oppression directly involves the political and economic power of our own country, we are in fact called to be a part of the struggle for liberation. As inhabitants of this incredibly wealthy nation, Christians will recognize that we are accountable to the poor and the disinherited of the earth. At the same time theologians of liberation should be reminded of the dangers that are present whenever religiously and morally imbued people dream of a new social order and commit themselves to bring that dream to reality. The more immediate and continuing need is for churches in every country to speak out against concrete instances of injustice and oppression, becoming a goad upon the conscience of those in power both in their own countries and throughout the world.

A Concluding Word

WE HAVE COVERED A LOT OF GROUND, and I am aware that we have often only hit the high spots. There is so much more that could be said, and many Christians who read these pages will think that many things not mentioned should have been. Be that as it may, enough has been presented to give the reader some idea of the dimensions of Christian belief. In this concluding word, at the risk of some repetition, I want to restate the invitation implicit in every consideration of the Gospel of Jesus Christ.

Summing up, briefly, we began by considering the cultural situation in which we live and the challenge it brings to the venture of Christian faith. We then looked at the relation of faith to theology and discussed the nature of theological reflection and the grounds on which it makes its assertions. Then we discussed four fundamental areas of Christian reflection: the meaning of human life, Jesus Christ, God, and the church. Each of these subjects addresses essential issues of human life—our identity as human beings, the struggle involved in the human predicament and the possibility of forgiveness and renewal through cross and resurrection, the question of human destiny and the hope by which we can live, and the basis for a community of reconciliation and renewal. We concluded with a consideration of the Christian life as a reflection of the faith professed by Christians.

Throughout our discussion we have been aware of a two-fold character to Christian faith. It involves, on the one hand, certain convictions concerning human life and its destiny in God. They can be stated as beliefs and endlessly scrutinized and dissected. One can pursue their implications and become absorbed in the rational activity we call theology. Yet at the same time these convictions are at root deeply personal. They are not simply ideas which can be abstracted from the lives which affirm them. Their very affirmation constitutes a venture of faith, a life-orientation which is quite consciously chosen. In other words, Christian beliefs are at the same time a commitment of trust which underlies one's whole life.

This means that the invitation to faith is a most comprehensive matter, the acceptance of which involves serious self-examination. It is important, however, that we avoid the notion that to accept the invitation results in a certain predefined way of life, as though there were but one way to be a Christian. Many different life-styles are found among Christians, each of which can be lived with integrity. But central to each is the recognition that the source and goal of one's life is revealed in the life of Jesus Christ. This fact embodies a call to be faithful, to be a follower.

Here is the challenge that is implicit in the invitation to faith. It is not only being grasped by the overpowering love of God expressed in the Gospel message. It is at the same time the invitation to discipleship, which is the challenge to let one's life be ordered by the cross. The cross becomes a powerful symbol which orients the lives of those who place themselves under that sign, uniting them with Christ in their willingness to share his ministry. Just what this means for each Christian is something for the individual to work out within the circumstances of his or her own life, receiving at the same time the support and nurture offered by the Christian community. But it cannot be done with anything less than seriousness of purpose.

The very nature of Christian discipleship draws believers together into a community of faith, the church, where worship together with fellow-believers expresses the commitment of faith and provides one with a sense of identity as a follower of Christ. Christian faith can hardly be imagined apart from community, for both the nature of the human predicament and the nature of faith bring us together. This is an essential part of the invitation. We not only need each other, but are called to serve and support each other.

As we noted, it is precisely this community character of Christian faith—the church, with all its failings—that provides the greatest problem for many people in coming to terms with Christianity. Some seek a Christian fellowship apart from the church, while others assume a personal but private faith which invariably withers away from the effects of isolation. Any version of Christianity which forsakes community is a distorted image of what it means to be a Christian and cannot long endure.

And so the invitation continues, communicated by the living witness of those who have already responded to it. In the pages of this book the invitation has been extended in a certain way, in which the reader has been invited to think through with me the meaning of Christian teaching as one possible life-commitment in a pluralistic world. In doing this we have acknowledged that there is no such thing as a totally disinterested exposition of the Christian faith. The work of theologians unfolds within the larger context of Christian life and witness and is their contribution to the ongoing interpretation of that witness. I would be the first to acknowledge that there is nothing in these pages concerning the Christian witness which makes it so rationally compelling, so logically overpowering, as to force the reaction, "Ah, but it *must* be true!" But then, there is no life-commitment which can make that claim. The believing response is more like that of Jesus' disciples when they were challenged to follow some other claim to the truth. They could only confess, "Lord, to whom shall we go? You have the words of eternal life" (John 6:68).

Annotated Bibliography

THE WORKS LISTED BELOW are but a few of many that could have been selected. They are for the most part of fairly recent origin, representing both Protestant and Roman Catholic authorship, and devoted either in whole or in part to subject-matter we have addressed in this book. Many of them are consciously directed to the lay person and avoid technical language, while others assume some theological background. But any reader of *Invitation to Faith* should be able to read them with profit.

I. FAITH AND THEOLOGY IN THE CONTEMPORARY WORLD

Bonhoeffer, Dietrich. *Letters and Papers from Prison* (ed. by E. Bethge, trans. by R. Fuller). New York: Macmillan, 1953.

This is an important work because of its impact on theology during the 1960s. Bonhoeffer reflects on theology in the coming age while sitting in a Nazi prison during World War II. The result is fragmentary but seminal ideas for "man without God."

Braaten, Carl. *The Future of God.* New York: Harper and Row, 1969.

One of the foremost representatives of the theology of hope in this country, Braaten discusses some of the major tenets of Christian faith from an eschatological perspective. It provides a good introduction to the futurist orientation.

Brown, Robert McAfee. *Is Faith Obsolete?* Philadelphia: Westminster, 1974.

Brown gives us an engaging treatment of religious faith from a Christian perspective, relating it to theology, history, knowledge, doubt, the moral life, and community.

Brown, Robert McAfee. *The Spirit of Protestantism.* New York: Oxford, 1961.

This is a lively presentation of Protestant theology for the general reader. As the author now acknowledges, the one subject that needs to be revised is his evaluation of Roman Catholicism in light of the many changes inaugurated by Vatican II.

Küng, Hans. *On Being a Christian* (trans. by E. Quinn). Garden City, N.Y.: Doubleday, 1976.

This is a remarkable book by a remarkable Christian. Küng is a Roman Catholic theologian from Germany, with a strong ecumenical consciousness, often critical of what he sees in his church. With impressive knowledge and refreshing honesty, Küng presents a comprehensive treatment of Christian belief in contemporary culture. He speaks eloquently to Christians of every tradition.

Micks, Marianne H. *Introduction to Theology.* New York: Seabury, 1964.

Convinced that "all Christians are under an imperative to be thinking Christians," Micks provides an excellent means for getting acquainted with Christian doctrine. She structures her approach according to the three resources or authorities in theology—scripture, tradition, and reason.

Porteous, Alvin. *The Search for Christian Credibility.* Nashville: Abingdon, 1971.

This is a presentation of Christian teaching in response to the erosions of secularism which the author sees as having created a crisis for Christian belief. He affirms the credibility of Christian faith, calling for a creative theological response to our times.

Thielicke, Helmut. *The Hidden Question of God* (trans. by G. W. Bromiley). Grand Rapids: Eerdmans, 1977.

The well-known German theologian addresses a number of topics and the questions they raise for Christian theology today —religion, church, man, truth, and God. He argues that the basic question underlying all others (boredom, alienation, loss of identity, power) is "the hidden question of God."

Tillich, Paul. *Dynamics of Faith.* New York: Harper and Row, 1957.

A wide-ranging discussion of faith, which Tillich defines as "the state of being ultimately concerned." He concludes with a discussion of the possibility and necessity of faith today.

Verhalen, Philip A. *Faith in a Secularized World*. New York: Paulist, 1976.

A Roman Catholic priest and college chaplain, Verhalen surveys the process of secularization and sees new possibilities for the understanding of God and the Christian message. He echoes Bonhoeffer's assertion that God is the "Beyond in our midst."

II. THE PROMISE AND PROBLEM OF HUMAN NATURE

Heschel, Abraham. *Who Is Man?* Stanford, Calif.: Stanford U. Press, 1965.

This is an eloquent affirmation on the part of the renowned Jewish scholar of the uniqueness and inherent worth of the individual. We become human and thus fulfill our destiny as we respond to the moral command that life (God) places upon us.

Moltmann, Jürgen. *Man: Christian Anthropology in the Conflicts of the Present* (trans. by J. Sturdy). Philadelphia: Fortress, 1974.

Moltmann finds the key to understanding human beings in the "Son of Man," the crucified Lord. In this sense human life drives us beyond the realm of biology, culture and religion in order to find its meaning and destiny in light of the cross.

Pannenberg, Wolfhart. *What Is Man?* (trans. by D. Priebe). Philadelphia: Fortress, 1970.

Our openness to the world as human beings leads us beyond our world, presupposing our dependence on God, our ultimate future. This theologian of hope presents a lucid account of human life in view of its destiny and in relation to the self and society.

Teilhard de Chardin, Pierre. *The Divine Milieu*. New York: Harper, 1960.

This book may serve as a good introduction to Teilhard. It reveals his deeply religious spirit in his discussion of the inner life of the individual, fusing psychology and theology in the description of the spiritual ascent. The "scientific," companion volume is his *Phenomenon of Man*.

Shinn, Roger L. *Man: The New Humanism (New Directions in Theology Today, Vol. VI)*. Philadelphia: Westminster, 1968.

Shinn discusses the emergence of a new appreciation of the human in the midst of the many anti-human developments of our "brave new world." The views of prominent theologians are discussed, as well as developments in the natural and social sciences which influence our understanding of the human.

III. THE MEANING OF JESUS CHRIST

Aulen, Gustaf. *Jesus in Contemporary Historical Research* (trans. by I. H. Hjelm). Philadelphia: Fortress, 1976.

The versatile Swedish theologian reviews here the work of representative scholars engaged in Jesus research since 1960. He concludes that remarkable agreement exists in regard to Jesus' central message about the kingdom of God, the content of his ethical teaching, and his behavior and relationship to various elements of the Jewish milieu. Aulen affirms biblical scholarship as having given us a trustworthy and defined picture of Jesus.

Barrett, C. K. *Jesus and the Gospel Tradition*. Philadelphia: Fortress, 1968.

The noted English biblical scholar here directs his attention to both the historical and theological questions concerning Jesus: What do we really know about Jesus? What did he really say and do? And what implications do the answers to these questions bear for our theological assessment of the exalted Lord?

Baillie, Donald. *God Was in Christ*. New York: Scribner's, 1948.

Though published thirty years ago, this book by the Scottish theologian is still well worth reading. Rejecting an either/or between the "Jesus of history" and the "Christ of faith," Baillie begins with Jesus of Nazareth and understands his uniqueness in terms of his total dependence on divine grace.

Bonhoeffer, Dietrich. *Christ the Center* (trans. by J. Bowden). New York: Harper and Row, 1966.

Consisting of student notes from his lectures and edited by his friend, Eberhard Bethge, this work brings out the centrality of Christ to Christian life and faith. Bonhoeffer stresses the reality of Christ in terms of his relation to us through the Word, sacraments, and faith-community.

Kasper, Walter. *Jesus the Christ* (trans. by V. Green). New York: Paulist, 1976.

Kasper provides a comprehensive treatment of the doctrine of

Jesus Christ, directed to students of theology. A Roman Catholic theologian, Kasper makes extensive references to both Catholic and Protestant works on this subject.

Knox, John. *The Humanity and Divinity of Christ*. New York: Cambridge, 1967.

Knox investigates the way in which the biblical writers dealt with the humanity of Jesus, whom they were proclaiming as resurrected Lord. He discerns a pattern which moved from the man Jesus to the resurrected Lord and Christ, and then to the establishment of his pre-existence which gave a particular character to the "divine-human problem."

May, William E. *Christ in Contemporary Thought*. Dayton: Pflaum, 1970.

This book serves the layperson well as an introduction to Christology. It surveys traditional thinking about Christ, the issues in historical research, and the views of twentieth century theologians, both Catholic and Protestant.

Robinson, John A. T. *The Human Face of God*. Philadelphia: Westminster, 1973.

Robinson argues that we must begin with Jesus the human being and express his divinity in terms of his humanity. He is the Son of God in his being "the representative man, who dies—and lives—for all." His uniqueness is in his vocation from God, which none of us could possibly duplicate.

IV. THINKING ABOUT GOD

Berger, Peter A. *Rumor of Angels: Modern Society and the Rediscovery of the Supernatural*. Garden City, N.Y.: Doubleday, 1969.

Berger responds to the alleged demise of the supernatural by finding within human experience certain "signals of transcendence" that point us beyond the natural order. As a sociologist who is also competent in theology, Berger brings a sociological and anthropological analysis to religious phenomena.

Cobb, John B., Jr. *God and the World*. Philadelphia: Westminster, 1969.

Cobb presents a process view of God as the most effective way of uniting God with the world and enabling us to affirm both

the world and God. He includes a discussion of evil and the relation of Christianity to religion.

Gilkey, Langdon. *Maker of Heaven and Earth.* Garden City, N.Y.:
Doubleday, 1959.

This is a comprehensive discussion of the Christian idea of
creation, which Gilkey relates to the physical sciences, philosophy,
and the language of myth and symbol. He succeeds in conveying
the profound illumination of human existence which is inherent
to a proper understanding of this teaching.

Knox, John. *Myth and Truth:* An Essay on the Language of Faith.
Charlottesville: The University Press of Virginia, 1964.

Knox writes concisely and clearly, providing a helpful discussion of the nature of mythological language and its indispensa-
bility to the expression of Christian belief.

Macquarrie, John. *Thinking About God.* New York: Harper and
Row, 1975.

The well-known Scottish theologian conducts a wide-ranging
exploration of this topic, considering first the problem of language
and criteria for truth in statements about God, then inquiring
into the meaning of belief in God and the grounds for such belief,
and concluding with a discussion of the thought of representative theologians on this subject.

Ott, Heinrich. *God* (trans. by Iain and Ute Nicol). Richmond:
John Knox, 1974.

Ott vigorously affirms God as Person who stands over against
us, illuminating our own personhood and what it means to be
human. An essential part of his argument is that belief in a personal God enhances our own self-understanding as human beings.

V. THE CHURCH TODAY

Brown, Robert McAfee. *Frontiers for the Church Today.* New
York: Oxford, 1973.

Convinced that the church exists for the world and not for
itself, Brown urges a "frontier existence" in which the church is
open and adaptable to the challenges of our time. Frontiers in
relation to inter-church life (the ecumenical challenge) as well
as in relation to various social realities are discussed.

Dulles, Avery, S. J. *Models of the Church*. Garden City, N.Y.: Doubleday, 1974.

From the works of both Roman Catholic and Protestant theologians, Dulles gleans five major types or models used to express the essential character of the church: as institution, mystical communion, sacrament, herald, and servant. He argues that a proper understanding involves dimensions of each model, rather than any one exclusively. He is critical of the institutional model, but recognizes its validity within limits.

Gilkey, Langdon. *How the Church Can Minister to the World Without Losing Itself*. New York: Harper and Row, 1964.

Gilkey addresses the church's relation to the surrounding culture, with its impact on the beliefs, behavior, experience and worship of the local church. He asks for a recovery of Transcendence in order for the church to be something more than a reflector of its surroundings.

Hendry, George S. *The Holy Spirit in Christian Theology*. Philadelphia: Westminster, 1956.

In a very balanced and evangelical fashion, Hendry addresses a number of problems in theology involving the doctrine of the Holy Spirit. The five chapters relate the Holy Spirit to Christ, God, Church, Word, and Human Spirit.

McBrien, Richard P. *The Remaking of the Church: An Agenda for Reform*. New York: Harper and Row, 1973.

McBrien, a Roman Catholic ecclesiologist, evaluates his church in light of the Second Vatican Council and sadly concludes that it has not fulfilled the promise set in motion by that Council. He advocates a thorough institutional reform in order to "ensure a convergence of the future we hope for and the future we will eventually settle for. . . ."

VI. THE LIFE OF FAITH

Bonino, José Miguez. *Doing Theology in a Revolutionary Situation*. Philadelphia: Fortress, 1975.

Bonino provides a very readable account of liberation theology in Latin America. This book serves as an excellent introduction to the subject.

Curran, Charles E. *New Perspectives in Moral Theology.* Notre
Dame, Ind.: U. of Notre Dame Press, 1976.

This well-known Roman Catholic moral theologian has contributed significantly to the rethinking of his church's moral
teachings. He provides an overview of Catholic moral theology,
reflects on the social mission and teaching of his church, and concludes with a discussion of several moral issues.

Fletcher, Joseph. *Situation Ethics: The New Morality.* Philadelphia:
Westminster, 1966.

No one in the field of theological ethics has argued the case for
a situational approach more consistently or insistently than Fletcher. In this exposition of his views, Fletcher argues love *(agape)*
as the one-and-only absolute for moral decision-making.

Gutierrez, Gustavo. *A Theology of Liberation: History, Politics,
and Salvation* (trans. and ed. by Sr. Caridad Inda and J. Eagle-
son). Maryknoll, N.Y.: Orbis, 1973.

This book is probably the most important single work in the development of Latin American theology of liberation, providing
both its context and its significance in relation to the rest of theology.

Macquarrie, John. *Three Issues in Ethics.* New York: Harper and
Row, 1970.

Macquarrie addresses the question whether there is a distinctive Christian ethic, and stresses its continuity with the "general
moral striving of mankind." He also discusses the shape of a
theological ethic for our time and the relation of religion and
morality. In elaborating on these questions he evaluates situation
ethics, the concept of natural law, and relates sin, grace and hope
to the subject of ethics.

Pike, James A. *Doing the Truth: A Summary of Christian Ethics*
(rev. ed.). New York: Macmillan, 1965.

Writing in a lucid and engaging style, Pike discusses the nature of Christian ethics as the expression of Christian convictions.
The latter part of the book addresses moral issues in political life,
sexual relations and business and professional life.

Notes

Chapter 1

1. The peculiar nature of statements concerning God will be discussed in Chapter 6. Our use of the word "cognitive" here means that a knowable reality independent of ourselves is being addressed, even though our statements about that reality are not to be understood in the same way as statements about something in our world.

Chapter 2

1. The development of critical methods of biblical study in the nineteenth century will be discussed below in Chapter 4.
2. In recent years the term "evangelicals" has been increasingly used by fundamentalists. However, there is also a significant movement of conservative Protestants today whose roots are in fundamentalism but who claim the title of evangelicals in an effort to move away from the strident literalism of fundamentalists. They are open to dialogue with other segments of the Christian community, while fundamentalists are not. They also demonstrate an appreciation of the church's responsibility in society beyond questions of personal morality.
3. These traditions are characterized more extensively in Chapter 8. Since Roman Catholicism and Protestantism are the major traditions in the Western world, we shall center our attention on them.
4. There is some difference among the three Christian traditions on what constitutes dogma. The Eastern (and Anglican) churches limit it to those teachings defined by the first seven ecumenical councils, and Protestants generally would agree though they tend not to use the word "dogma," referring to their own official theological statements as confessions of faith. Roman Catholics do not limit dogma to the early councils but see it continuing to be made in the official statements of councils and the *ex cathedra* or infallible pronouncements of the Pope up to our own time.
5. The Roman Catholic theologian, Karl Rahner, recognizes the universality of divine revelation in the receptiveness of human nature to

divine grace. Human beings are "open" to God because they have been created for him, and though many may never have heard of Jesus Christ, they may be "anonymous Christians" who by divine grace recognize their dependence upon God. Protestant theology, on the other hand, tends to be more pessimistic about the human capacity to respond to God and does not relate human nature and divine grace in the integrative, positive fashion of Rahner or Roman Catholic theology in general. Many Protestants would speak of a "hidden Christ" or a "universal Christ" who is apparent in the teachings of other religions where a sense of divine grace and trust in God is apparent.

Chapter 3

1. A good illustration of this attitude is seen in the remark of Dr. V. K. Ting, scientific head of the Chinese Geological Survey, to Teilhard de Chardin: "What is the point of tormenting yourself with the insolvable problems of the meaning of life, death and creation when these problems are beyond our understanding? True wisdom lies in acting as if such problems did not exist."
2. David Hollaz (1646-1737), quoted in Heinrich Schmid, *Doctrinal Theology of the Evangelical Lutheran Church,* third ed. (Minneapolis: Augsburg, 1961), p. 239.
3. Fundamentalist Christians would disagree with this interpretation of the story of the fall, insisting that it must be a historical event. They believe this not only because Christians in past centuries have regarded it as historical, but also because they think that if one allows that a particular narrative such as the fall is not historical, then a domino effect is set in motion and before we know it the historicity of Jesus himself would be challenged. This viewpoint fails to recognize the different kinds of material one finds in the Bible. Just because the story of the fall can be properly called myth, it does not mean that there is not also historical material in the Bible—as well as poetry, prophecy, legend, love songs, hymns, saga, parables, etc.
4. This calls to mind the publicity given in recent years to the "experiences" of those who had technically died but were brought back to life by the medical technology now available to us. Though some would speak of the "proof" we now have of life beyond death, theologians generally would be very hesitant to draw such a conclusion on the basis of the evidence cited, which can be interpreted in other ways as well.

Chapter 4

1. The controversy over the scientific study of scripture was traumatic for many Protestant churches during the nineteenth and early twen-

tieth centuries, giving rise to fundamentalism whose features we noted in Chapter 2. There was also resistance to critical biblical scholarship within the Roman Catholic Church, where the pope condemned it as one of the errors of "modernism." It was not until this century that Catholic biblical scholars began to seriously address and utilize critical tools of biblical study.

2. The designation "Christ" (from the Greek *christos*) is the title we use in English to convey the meaning of the Jewish Messiah as the one chosen of God to save his people. Though it is a title, common usage among Christians has turned it into a name: "Jesus Christ" instead of "Jesus, the Christ."

3. Various understandings of the cross as an act of atonement are discussed below, pp. 103ff.

4. Matthew 28, Mark 16, Luke 24, John 20-21. See also 1 Corinthians 15 and Acts 1.

Chapter 5

1. Gnosticism is a name given to a syncretistic religious philosophy that pervaded the ancient world at the time of Christianity's origin. There were a number of differing schools of thought, but all of them reflected a dualistic view of the universe, contrasting a good, eternal world of the spirit with an evil, temporal world of matter. Human beings belonged to both worlds, preexisting as souls that were now imprisoned in material bodies. Creation itself is a fall, and God, who could not be responsible for creation, is separated from the material world by spheres of being moving from pure spirit above to earthly matter here below. Through the acquisition of "knowledge" (gnosis) concerning the world of the spirit made possible by a redeemer-god, one could arrive at a saving vision of truth, but ultimate salvation awaited the escape from an evil body at death and returning to the world of immortality. The redeemer-god who conferred saving knowledge was understood as coming from the highest realm of being next to God himself, but not becoming "incarnate," which would be subjection to evil. It is difficult to say to what extent Christianity may have influenced Gnostic beliefs; it is clear that many Christian theologians regarded Gnosticism as a pernicious influence and a very real threat to the integrity of Christian faith.

2. This point must be noted, even though the categories of person and work have been traditionally distinguished (as I am doing also) in Christological discussion. After discussing Christ's person, we shall consider Christian interpretations of his work, or what was accomplished through him.

3. For example, some see the reference to Jesus as "Son of Mary" in Mark 6:3 as an acknowledgment that Joseph was not Jesus' father;

some see the words in John 1:13, "nor of the will of man," as carrying overtones of the virgin birth; and some see in Paul's reference
to Jesus as "born of a woman" in Galatians 4:4 a recognition of the
virgin birth.
4. It has been argued by Christians that Jesus was sinless by virtue of
his virgin birth. This argument is based on the assumption (going
back to Augustine) that original sin is transmitted through the
sexual act, a hereditary chain which is then broken in Jesus' case
where conception is occasioned by the power of the Holy Spirit. The
Roman Catholic dogma of the Immaculate Conception of Mary
(1854) then provided a further guarantee of Jesus' sinlessness. Most
theologians today, however, are no longer inclined to think of sin
and its transmission in such physical terms.
5. Jesus reads the human problem in just these terms in the Sermon
on the Mount: "Therefore I tell you, do not be anxious about your
life. . . . Look at the birds of the air: they neither sow nor reap nor
gather into barns, and yet your heavenly Father feeds them. Are you
not of more value than they? And which of you by being anxious
can add one cubit to his span of life? And why are you anxious
about clothing? Consider the lilies of the field, how they grow; they
neither toil nor spin; yet I tell you, even Solomon in all his glory
was not arrayed like one of these. But if God so clothes the grass
of the field, which today is alive and tomorrow is thrown into the
oven, will he not much more clothe you, O men of little faith?
Therefore do not be anxious . . . (Matt. 6:27-31a).
6. See his *God Was in Christ* (New York: Charles Scribner's Sons,
1948), pp. 171 ff.

Chapter 6

1. "The New Testament and Mythology," in H. W. Bartsch, editor,
Kerygma and Myth (London: SPCK, 1953), p. 10.
2. Female theologians are now making a significant contribution to the
theological task of the church. Among those who have addressed the
masculine and feminine issue in speaking of God are Mary Daly,
Beyond God the Father (Boston: Beacon, 1973) and Letty Russell,
Human Liberation in a Feminist Perspective—A Theology (Philadelphia: Westminster, 1974).
3. *The Ideal of the Holy* (New York: Oxford University Press, 1958),
pp. 12-13.
4. The speech of the apostle Paul at the Areopagus in Athens, recorded
in Acts 17, is instructive on this point. In order to make sense of the
Gospel for the Athenians, he begins by appealing to their own
apprehensions of the divine as expressed in one of their poets.
5. A similar view is expressed by Wolfhart Pannenberg: "The so-

called proofs for the existence of God show only that man must inquire beyond the world and himself if he is to find a ground capable of supporting the being and meaning of his existence . . . [the proofs] retain their significance as elaborations of the questionableness of finite being which drive man beyond the whole compass of finite reality. But they do not provide the answer to this question." *Basic Questions in Theology*, vol. II, trans. George H. Kehm (Philadelphia: Fortress Press, 1971), pp. 223 f.

6. If the doctrine is to be expressed mathematically, then given the proper understanding of the Trinity the appropriate equation would not be $1+1+1=1$, but $1x1x1=1$. The classical formulation of the Trinity was not "Father, *and* the Son, *and* the Holy Spirit," but the Father "through" the Son "in" the Holy Spirit.

Chapter 7

1. Cf. Chapter 3, "What the Idea of Creation Means," (Garden City, N.Y.: Doubleday and Co. [Anchor Books]), 1965.

2. The scientific genius, Isaac Newton (1642-1727), puzzled by the fact that the stars appeared to be stationary and not subject to the pull of gravity, proposed that the reason for this phenomenon was that God must be keeping them in position. In the seventeenth century a scientist could still make such a suggestion, but today his proposal would offend (or amuse) not only scientists but theologians as well!

3. Some scientists would claim that the world is eternal or ultimate, without a finite cause. Such a claim is difficult to prove on the basis of evidence, however. It betrays the philosophical position we call "naturalism," in which the world of nature is simply posited as ultimate. It is a philosophical belief.

4. There are actually two stories of creation in Genesis, the first in 1:1—2:4a, and the second in 2:4b-9. There are contradictions between them, but only if we take them as scientific accounts of the world's origin would there be any reason to make particular note of those differences. Both accounts are affirming the one essential truth: God is our creator.

5. See above pp. 28 ff.

Chapter 8

1. Protestants usually substitute the word "Christian" for "catholic," because the latter word is identified in their own minds with the Roman Catholic Church. The meaning of catholic is "universal."

2. The variety of doctrinal positions within Protestantism makes it difficult to describe a "Protestant" position on a particular issue without offending some Protestants. Our purpose here limits us to

painting in broad strokes without giving attention to differences to be found among various denominations.

3. It should also be noted that much of the disillusionment with preaching is due to the fact that many preachers are no longer preaching the Gospel. There are churches in which the message from the pulpit is more appropriate to a humanist society, containing a wealth of ideas on personal and social adjustment, peace of mind, community and national issues, etc., with no relation to the biblical witness. The sermon then becomes entirely dependent upon the gifts of the preacher, few of whom would warrant a weekly audience, year in and year out.

Chapter 9

1. See above, pp. 116 ff.
2. It is helpful to distinguish between ethics as the theoretical basis for moral behavior, involving the critical study of morality, and morality as the actual behavior patterns of individuals and groups in our society. The teachings of Jesus certainly provide a recognizable basis for a Christian ethic, but in regard to the question whether there is a specifically Christian ethic scholars argue about the relation of his teaching to the ethics of Judaism and the variety of interpretations subsequently given his teaching in the church. There is yet more variety of course in Christian morality, or the actual behavior of Christians, reflecting cultural and ethnic influences upon the church.
3. Not all situationists are saying exactly the same thing, of course. One of the more provocative and extreme exponents of this view is Joseph Fletcher, whose book, *Situation Ethics* (Philadelphia: Westminster, 1966), has provided a popular introduction to the subject.
4. We refer, of course, to the Roman Catholic Church which is overpoweringly dominant in the Latin countries. It has long been a sleeping giant that now in recent years has begun to stir. The impact it may yet exercise in behalf of personal freedom and more humane government could be profound. The principal advocates of liberation theology are Catholics, including Gustavo Gutierrez, Juan-Luis Segundo, Lucio Gera, and Hugo Assmann. Among Protestant representatives are Rubem Alves and José Miguez Bonino.
5. Gustavo Gutierrez, *A Theology of Liberation* (Maryknoll, N.Y.: Orbis, 1971), pp. 295 f.

Index